TEACHING FROM ZION - A RETROSPECTIVE

Collection 1 - 1980s

Joseph Shulam

Netivyah International

I dedicate this collection of my articles to all my family: my wife Marcia, the flag-ship of my life, the mother of my children, and Safta to my grandchildren. I also dedicate this collection to my daughter in law, Elizabeth, who put this project together, collecting all my articles from magazines since 1978. Upon reading the previous sentence, you might think I am redundant in how I write!

Yes, I affirm and reaffirm that my family deserves to receive this book's dedication . It will be a very interesting series, with a broad spectrum of material that will inspire and challenge the reader to learn more and be more inquisitive.

The articles were written for the magazine, Teaching From Zion, which started in 1978. Before 1978, articles were one sheet of paper written by Rabbi Moshe ben Maier, a dear Orthodox Jewish Disciple of Yeshua. He began writing in the 1920s. Moshe remained an Orthodox Jew 100% and a disciple of Yeshua the Messiah 100%. When Moshe died, I became responsible for publishing his prayer list every month. From this prayer list grew the Teaching From Zion magazine.

The Teaching from Zion Magazine has grown and spread around the world. There is a mailing list of over 3000 people who receive this publication. Each magazine deals with a specific topic, from food issues to the use of money in the New Testament, Yeshua in the Siddur (The Jewish prayer book), and Yeshua in the Talmud. The topics are chosen to be relevant for both Jews and

*Christians and deal with and answer
fundamental questions from brothers and sisters
around the world.*

*God bless all my family, especially Elizabeth.
Bless Netivyah Bible Instruction Ministry in
Jerusalem Israel and all its workers, men and
women, who have made the organziation a flag-
ship ministry for Jewish disciples of Yeshua, our
Messiah.*

*I also want to dedicate this book to the thousands
of people who have supported Netivyah's ministry
financially in Israel and worldwide. Supporters of
the Teaching from Zion Magazine and the
Hamotzi Food Program in Jerusalem in
cooperation with Jerusalem's city hall. To the
Supporters of the Purim gifts for the Israeli
soldiers each year. To the supporters of the
Sutdent Scholarship programs. Programs in the
plural as I together with contributions with Arab
disciples have supported several hundred Israel
and Arab Christians to study medicine in Israel
and Jordan. Thanks to all these people who have
given their love for Israel and for Jews and Arabs.*

*I dedicate this series to everyone, young and old,
rich and poor, who gave a dollar for the work of the
Lord through Netivyah in Israel and in the United
States via Netivyah International so named for
their purpose to spread our work from South
American to Finland and around several countries
in Asia.*

*I also dedicate this book to those who will continue
standing with Israel and supporting the Lord's
work in Israel and internationally. Both
ministries are symboitic twins that must work
together and spread the message of the restoration
of the church and promote unity and cooperation
each branch of the olive tree those who are natural
and those who are grafted into the olive tree by*

Yeshua's life, death and resurrection, and waiting eagerly for His speedy return to Jerusalem.

CONTENTS

FOR JEWISH EVANGELISM

FOREWORD

As Joseph approaches his 80th year of life on earth, one of his requests was to take all his articles written for the Teaching from Zion Magazine, produced and printed by Netivyah Bible Instruction Ministry in Jerusalem Israel and collate them together in a collection.

As I was working on this project, I couldn't help but be awestruck by the expanse of knowledge and subjects that Joseph wrote about over the course of 40 years.

I hope that the reader will appreciate the perspectives, wisdom, and education of Joseph Shulam and pass it on to another generation.

The body of believers in the Messiah Yeshua cannot afford to lose this knowledge as it seeks to continually restore the kingdom of God.

Elizabeth Shulam
Editor

PREFACE

My name is Joseph Shulam; I was born in Sofia, Bulgaria, in 1946, after my father returned to Bulgaria at the end of World War II. There are 15 years of difference between my sister Zelma and me. She was born in 1931, just before the rise of the Nazi Party in Germany, and I was born in 1946, just after the German Nazi Party supposedly died.

In 1947, my father, mother, sister, and I (I was one year old) boarded the ship Pan York and headed for Israel. The British mandate was still the governing document so called by the British (Palestine). My first memory was walking with one shoe off the Pan York and crying because the ship didn't land in a typical port but south of Haifa near an encampment called Padres Hannah.

My home was secular and anti-every-religion. My father hated every religion and looked at every religious person, a Jew or Christian or a Mongolian priest, as a superstitious idiot. This was my upbringing!

I attended a high school in Jerusalem, a Jewish high school with some of the finest teachers of my whole life. I must confess that throughout my life, I have had superb teachers, men and women of the highest possible caliber and scholarship. I can't say anything wrong about those teachers from kindergarten in Jerusalem, elementary school, and especially high school. In High School, Dr. Etai Zimran introduced me to the Hebrew Bible (The Old Testament) and the New Testament. We had plenty of Bibles in my home, including the Old and New Testaments. We used them, but not for reading! The Bibles were printed on good paper, and missionaries cast cases into our yard on Beth-Lehem Road 90 in Jerusalem. It was good paper, and we put it to good use.

My first assignment from my teacher, Dr. Zimran,

was to read the first ten chapters of the Gospel of Matthew and the first ten chapters of the book of Acts. My assignment was to write a paper on the beginning of Christianity. Well, after reading the ten chapters from the New Testament, the first time my eyes beheld the scriptures, I told Dr. Zimran that there is nothing "Christian" in the material I read. He responded, "Yeshua and his disciples were fine and good Jews," only after everything got messed up." For me, this was like the launch of the Santa Maria (one of the ships that discovered America).

I don't plan to write my autobiography here; I am writing it separately. My point is that I knew nothing about and had no religious affiliation with any religion. My parents' philosophy was that intelligent people don't believe in any God, much less in the God of Judaism and Christianity. Religion was for primitive and superstitious people.

Well, I have come a long way since that day. Several months after I handed my paper to Dr. Itai Zimran, I encountered a challenge. An American Missionary named Ernest Stewart challenged me. He lived in my neighborhood and had one of the finest cars in Israel, a big sky-blue Plymouth

1960 station wagon. He had a daughter and two sons. Even before he knew my name, he asked me a question: "What do you think about Jesus?" - Well, my answer was, "I don't think about Jesus at all!" Ernest Stewart said: "You must think about Jesus. First of all, he was the most important Jew who had ever lived. Second, because Jesus is your Messiah. Either he was the Messiah, or he is the biggest criminal and deceiver in the history of humanity. You have to make up your mind."

To cut this preface short, you all know by now that I did become a believer in Yeshua, the Messiah (in Greek "Jesus"). I have been leading and building the Netivyah Bible Instruction Ministry from the beginning of this magnificent Jewish Ministry with a community and a congregation in Jerusalem and disciples worldwide. And books written and published by the Hebrew University Press and Akademon. Other books self-published by Netivyah and the magazine Teaching from Zion started as a one-page typed prayer list and developed into a 30-page full-color semi-academic international magazine.

And now, in the autumn of my life, my daughter-in-law Elizabeth has collected most of my articles that were published in Teaching from Zion magazine into a collection on so many topics and issues and subjects that it will make an Irishman drunk even without taking a walk with Johnny Walker or Captain Morgan!

I hope you enjoy reading and maybe re-reading these articles covering every topic, from Apostle Paul's use of money to Yeshua in the Talmud.

God bless you, and please don't forget to visit the websites of www.Netivyah.org and www.netivyahinternational.org. — Both websites belong to Netivyah. One is older and is published in Jerusalem. The other is a new version of Netivyah USA, which focuses on international issues like the spread of antisemitism around the world and, with the big picture, addresses the ultimate most dangerous problems of the corruption of Christianity. We are both in Netivyah Bible Instruction Ministry in Israel and Netivyah International, committed to the same battles and encouragements for the Body of Christ.

Please stand with us and with Israel and help us provide spiritual, educational, and financial support for the needs of the international battles and specific humanitarian projects in Israel and other countries worldwide.

I bless you readers to read and learn, and feel free to ask questions through our websites.

THE FIRST ISSUE
OF TEACHING
FROM ZION

Teaching From Zion תורה מציון

"For out of Zion shall go forth the law,
and the word of the Lord from Jerusalem." (Isaiah 2,3)

Vol. 1--No. 1 – JANUARY 1981 (TEVET.5741)

"NETIVYAH"

The quarterly publication "Teaching from Zion" has been published for some years by Moshe and Aharah Ben-Meir. After Moshe Emmanuel Ben-Meir departed to be with the Lord, Aharah continued to publish the paper with great expertise. Now after "Netivyah", an association for the research of the Holy Scriptures, was established Mrs. Ben-Meir proposed for "Netivyah" to take charge of "Teaching from Zion".

J.S.

WHAT ABOUT A REVIVAL?

By The Late, MOSHE EMMANUEL BEN-MEIR

A. REVIVAL IS NEW LIFE

B. THE HOLY SPIRIT AND THE WRITTEN WORD.

1 Dec. 1980

C. THE TIME FOR REVIVAL IS PAST

LIVING IN ISRAEL

A LETTER FROM SALLY HINTON TO FAMILY AND FRIENDS IN THE U.S.

1 Dec. 1980

Dear Family and Friends,

Love,
Sally & Buck

FOR YOUR CHILDREN

SHALOM HAVERIM!

CAN YOU ANSWER THESE...?

1. Read John 14:6. Jesus is the .... truth, and ....
2. Isaiah 43:19. God will make a .... in the wilderness.
3. Psalm 86:11. We must be taught the .... of the Lord.

MAY WE ALL BE ON THE WAY OF THE LORD!   NETIVYAH

VOLUME 1, NO. 1. JANUARY 1981

The quarterly publication "Teaching from Zion" has been published for some years by Moshe and Ahuvah Ben-Meir. After Moshe Emmanuel Ben-Meir departed to be with the Lord, Ahuvah, his wife continued to publish the paper with great expertise. Now after "Netivyah", an association for the research of the Holy Scriptures, was established Mrs. Ben-Meir proposed for "Netivyah" to take charge of "Teaching from Zion".

The first issue of "Teaching from Zion" in 1981 is also the first that "Netivyah" is publishing. Since not all of our readers are familiar with "Netivyah", it would be appropriate to introduce our association. "Netivyah" means, in Hebrew 'the Way of the Lord'. It is a recognized, non-profit organization, dedicated to the study and teaching of the Scripture in light of their Jewish and historical background. The major objectives of "Netivyah" are to promote an understanding between Jews and Christians, and the restoration of the teachings and practices of the first century church. In addition Netivyah has the plan to start a group which eventually we'll develop a Messianic settlement.

We hope that this publication will be instrumental in two important areas. First, we would like to inform our readers of the work and efforts of "Netivyah". Second, "Teaching from Zion" can be an important organ for the teaching and encouragement of the restoration of Messianic faith as in the first century.

This is a publication which could become an important tool both for our brothers in the world, and for the Messianic movement.

But, we will need your prayer support, and financial support in order to continue teaching and working for the Messiah — even to publish this very publication.

Read it, praise the Lord, and find room in your heart to support it both in prayer and finance.

****

What About A Revival?

By The Late MOSHE EMMANUEL BEN-MEIR

In whatever meeting one attends, one constantly hears the word: Revival. Preachers emphasize it. Teachers teach about it, evangelists preach it, and many pray for it; yea, we all need it.

What is a revival?
How does it come?
How long need we wait for it? What are its signs and accomplishments?

•   REVIVAL IS NEW LIFE

The Hebrew has two words for revival. The Bible word T'chiyah which is related to Chayim (life), and means resurrection, and the modern Hitorerut, which means awakening.

A classic Scripture is Hosea 6:1-3.
In verse 1 the prophet calls upon Israel to return unto the Lord, and makes four promises:

•He will heal what He has torn
•He will bind up what He has broken;
•He will revive us, and
•He will raise us up that we may live.

In verse 3, he calls upon them to press on to know the Lord, and promises that He will come on us:

•As the showers, and
•As the spring rains that water the earth.

The same prophet speaks again about the reviving of Israel and likens it to a revival of corn which shall be brought about by the Lord being to them as the dew. As a result Israel shall blossom as the rose, and strike roots as the cedars of Lebanon, and blossom as the vine (Hos. 14:5-8).

One of the Psalmists relates revival to calling upon the name of the Lord (Ps. 80:19b).

Another related it to rejoining in the Lord (Ps

85:7)

King David relates it to release from Tribulation and the power of enemies (Ps. 135:7, 143:11-12)
Revival is a blessing reserved for the low and broken hearted, says Isaiah 57:15.

The agent of revival is the Word of God and His precepts (Ps. 119:50,93).

The Holy Spirit is the chief agent (2 Cor. 3:6).

B. THE HOLY SPIRIT AND THE WRITTEN WORD.

Apart from these, revival is impossible. The Holy Spirit alone causes no revival. The Word alone causes no revival. The Holy Spirit and the Word cause revival.

Revival is designed in a very special sense for people who have been baptized and received the Holy Spirit. Among the millions of drowsy, sleepy, dead "believers", there is a good majority of dead "Pentecostal believers". These became dead because they occupied themselves with the "Holy Spirit" only, as if the Holy Spirit was the final purpose of the life of faith. The "Holy Spirit" so filled them that it, a) drove the Messiah out of the center of their life and longing, and b) blinded their eyes to the full contents of the Word, so all they cared to read were those passages which speak about the Holy Spirit and "tongues". The agent became the Lord. The means became the end.

A "holy" spirit which does not magnify the Messiah, which does not draw full and complete attention to Him, is in reality an unholy "holy" spirit. The "tongues", the "healings", the "signs" and "wonders" originating from it are intended to drug them, so that believing they have the true, they praise and deify the lie. A spirit which does not keep a person humble and lowly, loving and affectionate, which does not purify the Jew from despising the goi (gentile) and the goi from antisemitism or Jew-hate of any form, is not the Holy Spirit.

The decisive "sign" of the fullness of the Holy Spirit is love: not "tongues", not the gift of "healing", of "teaching", or of "commanding demons" or giving to church, mission, or community charity, although these are important.

We need revival because we do not love one another, because the **love of God** is not in us and does not drive us as it did the Master every minute of His life on earth.

How many are there in the churches, assemblies, and in the families who understand what they read in the Book of God? How many know what the redeemed life is all about. How many rejoice, like King David, to run in the way of God's commandments? How many delight in harmful pleasures? The people are sick and the ministers keep them going by "religious injections" of many brands. They mesmerise them and inject into their souls a confidence which is not based on biblical truth, and in time of crisis bursts as a soap bubble.

Revival will change all these.

C. THE TIME FOR REVIVAL IS PAST

The great apostasy is in process and gaining ground from hour to hour. Apostasy means falling away from the truth to believe the lie. A Spirit of deception is now in the lead, and God sent this spirit of deception. It is impossible to be filled with the Spirit of Truth and the spirit of deception in the selfsame hour. Babylon is destined for destruction and not for redemption. No revival can have any effect on the scarlet clad female from whose golden wine cup all the nations of the world tasted, drank, and became drunk. There is no renewal for her. Revival may be possible for the people of God which are in her, but only after they obey the summons to get out of her. There is no revival promises for the people who refuse to get out of her. They are doomed to partake of her sins, and drink the cup of wrath meant for her God has no respect for ecumenic and charismatic movements who disobey the call for total separation and obedience.

Those who will dare to go out of Babylon will be blessed and revived, and be transformed and taken up to meet the Lord in the air, when He shall return from His position at the right hand of the Majesty on high to ascend the throne of His father David.

****

Living In Israel

E. Yitzhak

This article is intended for two types of people:

•Those intending to immigrate to Israel, being Jewish and believers in Yeshua (Jesus) the Messiah.

•Those who feel they ought to pray for Israel and for those concerned in the spiritual warfare there. When God has led a Jewish believer (many times personally) back to the promised land, this is a prime factor that helps him remain there. However, I've seen a number of these kind of people go back. That some say "it is God's will"; it's hard for me to believe, but also hard to contest. Maybe they grew weary in this spiritual desert land and lost the vision that Israel will be saved. Who's to know?

Israel, today, is no easy place to settle down. I say this after being an immigrant unceasingly in Israel for 8 years. Now, I have actually bought a house in Upper Nazareth. I have also married a Russian immigrant, also a believer in Yeshua the Messiah, and have had a daughter born here. Israel is no easy place, even for the Israeli. Nowadays, thousands leave their native Israel to live in the more affluent west. Why are they, the native Israelis, leaving? It can't be because of terrorists or because of war lurking on the horizon. From my experience, these only make the attachments to the country stronger. The answer lies not in any external shaking, as Israel has proved victorious (to God be the glory!) in all four of her wars and has suppressed terrorism, even more than Europe has. The answer lies in an internal shaking from within. Israel's morale has been steadily declining, especially so in the last two years. Even three or four years ago, there was a feeling of helping each other, which now has deteriorated more and more, and has been replaced with unrestrained selfishness. There are new strikes practically every week, inflation over 150%, and more crime. Now, the Minister of Religion is to be put on trial for taking bribes. Simcha Erlich, the last Finance Minister was forced to resign and replaced by Horowitz, who has only worsened the plight of our economy and was also faced to resign. The Housing Minister, David Levi, is under bombardment for all the abandoned apartments not used even for years. Many are delayed months untold, for the lack of housing. Immigrants often meet indifference, apathy and even rudeness in the Ministry of Immigrant Absorption.

Believers in Israel have all this pressure plus the spiritual pressure. Anyone who is open in the least about his faith faces open mockery, accusations that he is a missionary (a dastardly crime!), blasphemous remarks about our Savior, and sometimes physical violence individually, or to the believers worshiping together. Because of such spiritual pressures, believers in Israel are closer knit together. Whether it be harassment in the army, hardship or losing one's job, or other attacks from the enemy, there is a special encouragement in fellowship. For "wherever sin abounds, grace abounds even more."

For the prospective immigrants, they'll not only be warned about what to expect but should keep in mind the spiritual rewards to look forward to, not only in the life to come but also in this life — in Israel. As for the interceders, they will be able to pray in knowledge and more specifically. Israel will be saved as mentioned in Zechariah 12:10-14 by the Lord Himself. Not by "hit and run" "preachers''.

Many believers rooted here have tried patiently to reason and show salvation to their fellow Jews. Some of these precious brothers have grown weary in their work and their vision has dimmed. Rumor has it that there are hundreds who believe secretly in Israel.

One will never know how much fruit he has borne, until the Master of the Harvest comes. Paul heard a cry from Macedonia in a vision "Come over here and help us!" May the cry of your brothers and sisters in Israel come to you: Come over here (immigrate) and help us (prayer).

****

A Letter From Sally Hinton To Family
And Friends In The Usa

1 Dec. 1980

Dear Family and Friends,

We had such a nice experience a few weeks ago that I want to share it with all of you. On November 21st & 22nd we attended a seminar for Jewish believers in Jerusalem, staying at the Finnish School which had very modest but clean and pleasant accommodations. The seminar was planned and led by Joseph Shulam and several other of the Jewish believers living in Jerusalem. Many other such seminars are planned for the future.

Many of you know Joseph, a Jew with a very strong faith in Yeshua the Messiah, and his wife Marcia who have dedicated their lives to bring Yeshua to the Jewish people in this land. Their home is always open to any who want to come and learn. They do a lot of helping, understanding and loving those about them. Marcia is like a daughter to us. She and her parents spent many hours with our family when Marcia was a teenager. June and Horace live near Carlisle, Pa.

The theme at the seminar was "The Faith of our Fathers" (Abraham, Isaac, Jacob). It began with registration at 4:30 on Friday afternoon. At 5.00 we began the first session with a moving song period, led by Zvi and Freddie. I didn't understand the words of many of the Hebrew songs, but we did feel the mood, the sincereness, and complete happiness of these Jewish brethren. What a thrill to be a part of this witness!

After the singing Joseph spoke on the life and faith of Abraham. He brought out so many points I had never considered on Abraham's faith. Joe is such a scholar and has a wonderful knowledge of the scriptures. I'm sure I missed some of the translation; we had a young man that quietly translated for our little group of "English speaking only" people.

By the time we met in the dining room for dinner, we were approx. 60 in number. The blessing for the meal was done by an elderly Jewish man. How wonderful to see, even men who have been waiting many years for a Savior, to realize and openly admit that Yeshua did come, and is indeed their Savior. To see the young admit this is wonderful, but to see this elderly gentleman, whose beard was white and face showing the lines of many years, was a thrill beyond measure. At 8:30 we met again for a "Messianic Culture Evening". There were couples who sang, some gave readings. We felt the highlight of the evening was when Joseph asked a group of Russian believers if they had anything to contribute. They sang so very beautifully two Russian songs. They were so appreciated that the people clapped for more. There were two men about 60 years old, a young man and a couple with a daughter, translated a lot into Russian from the Hebrew for her parents.

We ate dinner with a young couple on Saturday. She was Russian, her husband American, both Israelis now. She told us there were many Russian believers in Israel.

Another told us that if all the Russian believers in Jerusalem would have come to the seminar they would have filled the room.

Many of the songs sung during the evening were direct quotes from Psalms, Isaiah, Jeremiah, etc., and gave us some idea of what singing in the early N. Testament church must have been like.

We also met several young American Jews who are living in Israel, trying to witness Jesus. Some are living as volunteers on kibbutz.

On Saturday (Shabbat) we met for a period of worship and study at 9:30 a. m. Salim, a young man from Ramat Hasharon (we live in that community), gave a lesson on Abraham's hospitality. I never knew so much could be learned by that chapter.

At 10:30 we separated into classes; Buck and I chose the only one in English. Freddie had a very good lesson on "The Faith and Deeds of our Fathers". We had dinner at 12:30, followed by a free period of informal fellowship. Buck and I were impressed by the complete happiness and excitement about their
faith in Jesus, Their willingness and desire to

share it with others renewed in me a spirit to be more open in my faith. So many times I know I am guilty of "quenching the Spirit .

At 2:00 p.m. we met for the closing session and there was an elderly gentleman from Russia who missed the Friday evening cultural session. (We were over 70 at the session). This man was 82 years old, with snow white hair and beard, and spoke only Russian. He asked if he could sing a song; I think it was a direct quote from Jeremiah. He did it so beautifully and with deep emotion.

We thank God every day for the opportunities we have here in this land. It's experiences like this seminar that make it easier to bear the separation of our parents, our children and grandchildren, the rest of our family and friends.

Love, Sally & Buck

****

For Your Children

SHALOM HAVERIM!

Welcome to our first get-together by means of "Netivyah's" newspaper , the name Netivyah means "the way of the Lord".

Meet Barry. He is on the way of the Lord. Barry is in Netivyah. Barry is interested in soccer, baseball, guitar. . . Barry would like to be a pen pal with anyone who will write to him.
Address: Barry Shulam.
P.O. Box 8043
Jerusalem
Israel

CAN YOU ANSWER THESE. . .?

·Read John 14:6. Jesus is the truth.

·Isaiah 43:19. God will make a way in the wilderness.

·Psalm 86:11. We must be taught by the Lord.

THE ARTICLES
OF JOSEPH
SHULAM

COLLECTION 1

The 1980s

CHUTZPAH

From Teaching From Zion, Issue No. 5
September 1982

The word "Chutzpah" is probably the most characteristic word to describe the Israeli. In England "Chutzpah" would be translated as "Cheek", in modern American slang it would be "Attitude" - in older American slang it was just plain "Brass."

In Israeli talk, however, "Chutzpah" still needs to be explained - or should I say experienced.

When a beggar on the streets of Jerusalem is given a 50€ coin and he asks you: "What are you so poor? A Dollar you already can't give? This you might say is "Chutzpah". One could come to the conclusion that "Chutzpah" is a terrible thing - an uncivil attitude and probably the above example might reinforce this feeling. But let us see "Chutzpah", at least for a moment, in a different light. "Chutzpah" is that attitude that says to those that say it can't be done, "I know it can - and it will be done".

It is the attitude that when everyone in a

congregation says "Amen" - some with the "Chutzpah" would say why "Amen?" This is the force that has driven people to great heights when they have every "good reason" to stay flat on the ground . Israel, from the beginning of its modern statehood has been marked with the character of having much or, or one might say, too much "Chutzpah."

In our small organization called "Netivyah" (the Way of the Lord) we have had to admit that it is only the vision and the force of faith in the Messiah that has given us the courage or shall I say the "Chutzpah" to desire such great things as a Messianic Center of Learning in Jerusalem and a Jewish Moshav in the Galilee that will be populated with people who believe in the New Testament. It was this kind of vision and this attitude that took me and the family to the United States this summer. The support which I am receiving was about to end.

Although we had large attendance in our services and more teaching to do than time, we do not see any additional leadership emerging. In short, I could say that we had "good reasons" to be giving up and going to the U.S.A. and all this especially now when funds for evangelism are so difficult to raise. However, here comes the "Chutzpah."

In place of giving up, we took up the challenge of going to the United States and raising funds for a Messianic Center of Learning in Jerusalem, and for a car, and also the on-going support and living allowance for the Shulam family. As most of our readers know, the Finnish people have already contributed large amounts of money to "Netivyah" through the good offices of Paavali Toivio and his travel organization and the brothers in Israel have put these funds toward a building in Jerusalem. However, we still have to raise the sum of 250,000 U.S. dollars

In order to buy the most modest facility that would serve our needs. (You Should know that Israel is the most expensive place to buy property and Jerusalem would be the highest place in Israel. An acre of land in a modest quarter in Jerusalem would be over 75,000 dollars.)

The Lord God of Israel was good to our "Chutzpah" of faith. During this last summer I have traveled about 50,000 miles all over the United States. From this travel we believe that the Lord has really blessed us.

The funds to replace our car have been received, our oversight for the next three years has been promised by good brethren in California, and we have a number of people and congregations that will have special contributions for the building fund.

In addition to all these physical blessings, we have also been blessed by two spiritual attitudes that we have seen in the U.S. and which we believe to be all over the western world of Christianity. One is the attitude of wanting to know - I found people all around the country that really want to know the truth and are not fearful to find out.

It is true that this is not as widespread an attitude as those who would just want to keep the status quo and would not learn anything different from what they are used to even if Jesus would come to teach them.

But it still was an encouragement to see that there are many people who still would come and search the scriptures to find out what God wants from them.   The second thing that made me happy spiritually was that many Christians are starting to realize that they need the Old Testament in order to understand the New. And that the New Testament is not really a new religion that was started by Jesus Christ who was once Jewish and when he grew older and wiser converted to Christianity and condemned everything that went on before him in Judaism. I think that more and more people in the West see that the Antinomian, rootless new religion which has grown out of New Testament Christianity, is not what was taught by the Gospels and the Apostles. I found that many want to go back and restudy the Word of God and find life and life more abundantly in doing the will of God. In short we were really blessed by our "Chutzpah" and found that it is God's will that we shall continue to work among the people of Israel to comfort them, to love, teach, and to wait for the return of our Lord and Savior Yeshua Son of David.

Now this is enough about America, let me tell you about what was going on this summer in Jerusalem. The whole summer the brethren in Jerusalem met regularly every Saturday night and Sunday afternoon or break bread. They shared the responsibility of preaching and they continued to give of their means for the on-going of the Lord's work. It was a difficult summer for them because they have really known only one person who was the "leader" and now they had to be on their own.

I must say that with minor problems which came up, the congregation has come through the summer. However, it is clearly evident that we are still not finished with our job - if we would leave right now the congregation would not last and be faithful for long. We saw this summer that the most important thing which we can
do now is to train young leadership which will keep the congregation pure doctrinally. I guess that people did not change much since the time Paul wrote his letters to the church at Corinth. However, I really feel that the experiences of this summer will serve to strengthen the brothers in Israel in the long run.

You see now they know how easy it is to be led by the Devil down the primrose path. The Scriptures teach us to vigilance and watchfulness because the "Evil One" does not rest or stop looking to make a Christian sin.

The Lord has blessed us with a secretary - Ms. Ruby Little. She comes from Portland, Oregon where she has served Dr. J. P. Sanders for almost ten years.

We believe that our reports and correspondence will improve greatly with Ruby. She will start to study Hebrew on the 11th of October and will take an active part in the life of the Christian young sisters in Israel. The Eastside congregation in Portland will be her supporting congregation.

Mr. Fred Edelstein will also be working part time with the church in Jerusalem. Fred is an architectural designer and has a lovely wife and two daughters. He moved from Nazareth to Jerusalem especially to work with the congregation. We need to pay Fred's rent in Jerusalem as compensation for his work with the congregation. We still do not have the $350 per month to pay this rent. We hope that you will pray with us about this need.

October 21st, Lord willing, I will be going to Finland with Sister Ahuvah Ben-Meir as translator. We have been invited by Brother Paavali Toivio to hold some teachings about Israel and the early church. We ask all of you to pray for The Finnish people are one of the most interested in Israel and in the message of the New Testament.

The subjects which I hope to speak about are: "Grace and Faith in the Old Testament - John 1:17"; "Israel - Why Should it Exist"; "What must we do to be saved in the 20th Century"; "Second Generation Christians"... etc. After ten days in Finland, I have an invitation to go to Germany and teach there for two weeks. I think that these trips are important but we do not want to neglect our life and work in Israel.

The brothers and sisters in Israel are now, with all of Israel, on the crossroads of history - we must teach the Living Messiah now.

Help, Israel Return to its Roots in the Messiah.

HAS GOD REJECTED
HIS PEOPLE?

From TFZ. Volume 1, no. 7, March 1983.

Recently, a dear sister from the United States sent me photocopies of pages from Max King's book and also an article "**Zealots at Masada and Zealots at Jerusalem.**" I was amused to see people, who claim to be members of the "New Testament Church" and "to speak where the Bible speaks", give an answer so diametrically opposed to the answer Paul gives in Romans 11:1,

> *"I ask, then, has God rejected His people?*
> *By no means! I myself am an Israelite..."*

I'm quite aware that the problem of Israel is not a simple one. Most of the people who seem to show support for Israel are walking the primrose path of protestant traditional theology. However, between the theological excess of the millenarians and the words of Paul in Romans 1 there is not necessarily a connection. We ought not to fall trap to the traditional anti-Jewish feelings of "Christianity".

This feeling is well summarized in the words of Erasmus of Rotterdam, "If it is Christian to hate Jews, then we are all good Christians."

However, we are all so quick and careful to point out that, as disciples of the Messiah, we love the Jews. As a matter of fact, some of my best friends are Jews - my doctor, lawyer, and jeweler.

Let me share with you some basic guidelines for the understanding of Israel and the Jewish problem in light of the New Testament:

1. Salvation, for all men, is always on a personal basis of faith and obedience to God's word (i.e. it cannot be on a national basis).

2. Just because salvation is on a personal basis of faith does not mean that the Almighty has stopped dealing with nations or keeping His promises. (Is not the U.S.A. "one nation under God". Do you believe that God had anything to do with the establishment of the United States or with Finland? See Romans 13:1-4.)

3. Election and salvation are independent of each other. God chose Israel and said:

"The Lord your God has chosen you to be a people for His own possession, out of all the peoples that are on the face of the earth.... It is

*because the Lord loves you and is keeping the
oath which He swore to your father...." Deut.
7:6,8. However, to the same generation in the
wilderness He said: "I swore in my anger that
they should not enter my rest". Psalms 95:11.*

God elected Israel but they were not all saved
and they did not all take benefit of the election
of God. However, Romans 11:28 states in a clear
way that although hated concerning the Gospel,
they are still elect for the Father's sake.

4. The dispensational ideas which have
conquered the evangelical Christians have
been the major exponents of pre-
millennialism. Is dispensationalism an early
church doctrine or did Darby first come up
with it and Schofield make it popular? Why
should we, as first century Christians, hold any
different attitude from Paul, Peter, or James
about Israel? Paul best expressed his attitude
toward Israel in Romans 9:2-5.

*"I have great sorrow and unceasing anguish
in my heart. For I could wish that I, myself,
were cursed and cut off from Christ for
the sake of my brethren, my kinsman, by
race. They are Israelites, to them belong the
sonship, the glory, the covenants, the giving
of the Law, the worship, and the promises;
to them belong the patriarchs, and of their*

race according to the flesh is the Christ who
is over all be blessed forever. Amen."

5. The concept that has become prevalent in our Western Christianity that everything concerning the church and the family of God started at Pentecost is a concept that does not take into account the full picture presented by God's word. God did not start all over again at Pentecost. What happened at Pentecost was that which God had expected, prophets had prophesied, and people waited for. At least, some of the Jews were waiting for The Messiah, (Luke 2:25; Mark 15:43). **The apostles repeatedly taught and claimed that they were preaching that which was from the beginning, that which God had declared to Abraham, and that which was before the foundations of the world, not something which was the result of a mistake which God had made when He chose the Jewish people to carry the flag of salvation and to bring to the earth, the Savior, the Messiah.** (See Romans 1:2, 15:8; Acts 26:6,7; Eph. 1:4; Acts 2:23; Hebrews 1:1)

Let us consider this scenario with you. Let us say that God elected the Jewish people and expected them to do a job and that they, as a nation, did not live up to God's expectations and did not accomplish that job. Therefore, God had to choose somebody else, the Gentiles, to come and to do the same job which the Jews were chosen to do. Would that not make God one who has made a mistake? Would this mean that God was imperfect in His choice of the Jewish people? Even worse than this, would that not make God a liar? God has promised that the people of Israel would be His election to the end of the world. (Read Jeremiah 31:35-37; Isa. 54:8-14;) Jeremiah says, "that as long as the sun is in the heavens and the moon is in the skies God will not reject His chosen people." By all this, **I don't mean that the Jews have any special privileges regarding salvation or in regard to benefits that they can receive and Gentiles can't.** I do mean to say that God still has a job and task for them in history.

A task which is not only to bring the Messiah but to accept the Messiah themselves as Romans 1 clearly states that they will. Of course, we all know that this will not happen without faith and it will not happen without their obedience to the Gospel, just like everybody else. It is, the choice, of God's election, and a proof that God did not make a mistake. The Gentiles or the Jews are not better than each other but are, together, bound both in unbelief and in belief. In addition to all this, if God did not keep His word to the Jewish people, even though they were not always faithful, what guarantee do the Christians of this world have that God will keep His word to them? Jesus, as the Messiah, vindicated the election of Israel by being born in Israel, to a Jewish mother, in Bethlehem; fulfilling that which God has foretold by the mouth of His prophets. He was Israel par-excellence. If one reads the servant passages in Isaiah one finds immediately that the servant is called Israel, Jacob. He is the one who is the suffering servant of Isaiah 53 and He is the one who bore our sins and our transgressions and by whose Stripes are healed . Of course, we all realize that Jesus is useful and that we h a v e witnessed His crucifixion not as a Huguenot or Lilliputian but as King of the Jews. It would also be of benefit for us to read passages in the book of Acts where Paul witnesses of his own faith . Like in chapter 24:14-17, that he believes all that is written in the law and in the prophets. In Philippians and in Acts Paul continually states in the present tense, "I am a Jew" not "I was a Jew" but "I am a Jew". Who said that we stopped existing? We are people who breathe and eat and create and compose and invent and have identity. We have received, handed down to us, through the centuries the love of God even in our diaspora. God is still waiting for us to respond, by faith, and to believe in

the Messiah. We have to work hard and take
our faith to Israel as a proof of the great love
which God has loved the world not excluding
His very children in the flesh. As Jews, we are
incomplete without Jesus as our Messiah. However, that incompleteness does not mean that
we don't exist.

6. There is no Biblical grounds to hold the
position that God has rejected Israel or that He
is finished with them and no longer interested
in their salvation. The contrary is true. God
has not rejected His people (Rom. 11:1, 25-29)
and anyone who holds to such a doctrine is
contrary to the Holy Scriptures of God and
contrary to the very promise that God has
made to the church that they will be grafted
into the olive. This was the point which Paul
made when he spoke about the Gentiles in
Ephesians 2:11-22. Before they received Jesus
Christ the Son of the living God, the Messiah,
they were without God, without hope, outside
the commonwealth of Israel. Now that they
have received the Messiah, they have become
fellow citizens of the same city and members
by implication of the commonwealth of Israel.
I don't say this to aggrandize myself or the
Jewish race or the Jewish people but I do say
it because it is a Biblical doctrine and because
2,000 years of "Christian antisemitism" must

come to an end before the church, the believers, the Christians can provoke Israel to jealousy. The great restoration preachers all held by and believed the promises of God. All wanted to return back and be like the early church. It is significant that we should restore also the attitudes of the early church toward Israel, unashamedly, and proclaim that God is still interested in the Jewish people and in their salvation by whom, through whom, and for whom Christ shed His blood.

In summary, I want to repeat and say that we ought not to accept the anti-Semitic theological grounds that have driven " Christianity " into such bestiality as we have witnessed in our generation. Germany, of our generation, was the same Germany that Martin Luther came from and that the reformation started from. It is the same Germany that was so influential in the beginning of the return of Christianity back to a more Biblical faith. We ought not to forget this point. The Holocaust happened in Germany and it was going on while the people were going to their Lutheran churches to pray to a Jew on a cross. It could happen again to those that are limiting the love of God just to their own family and race. Let us open up and receive the word of God, rightly dividing in the light. If we are going to truly restore the family and the church which Yeshua, Jesus the Christ, established in the first century we must do so in light of what the prophets of Israel have spoken many centuries earlier all the way back to Abraham. Let me conclude a few lines from Augustine that will show his mind as regards to the Jews: "Let us preach to the Jews, whether we can, in a spirit of love, whether they welcome our words or spurn them. It is not for us to boast over them as broken branches. Rather let us consider by whose grace, and with what loving kindness, and into what kind of root it was that we were grafted." One does not have to be a millenarian to see that God is keeping His promises. I am not a pre or post millennialist. I am a Jew who believes that Jesus is the Messiah, Son of God.

I hope you are my brother.

Joseph Shulam

P.S. If there are questions about the article or our faith and actions would you be so kind and act according to Matthew 18:15. "If thy brother shall trespass against thee, go and tell him his fault between thee and him alone...." I promise to answer every letter.

P.S.S. Questions might come up about passages like Gal. 3:1-5 , 19 - 4:20, 5:2-4 or Hebrews 9:9-15 etc. . If you read these passages you do not find anything about the people of Israel - only about the legal aspects of the old covenant.

A list of suggested books:

1. Jacob .M Myers. Grace and Torah, (Fortress. 1975)

2. Gerard S. Sloyan. Is Christ the End of the Law?, (Westminster. 1978)

3. Daniel P. Fuller. Gospel and Law- Contrast or Continuum? (William P. Eerdmans Publishing Co. 1980)

"HEAR, O ISRAEL, THE LORD OUR GOD, THE LORD IS ONE. AND LOVE THE LORD YOUR GOD WITH ALL YOUR HEART, AND WITH ALL YOUR SOUL ,AND WITH ALL YOUR MIGHT. AND THESE WORDS WHICH I COMMAND YOU TODAY, SHALL BE UPON YOUR HEART." (DEUT. 6:4-6)

GOING ONWARD AND UPWARD

From Teaching from Zion , Vol 1 No 8, July 1983

Since May 17, 1983 much of our life and work has been wrapped around the new building that Netivyah purchased in Jerusalem. We have collectively worked, cleaned, and basically refurbished the interior of the building in order to make it suitable and useful for our purposes . Almost everybody in the congregation has pitched in and given of his time, talents, and finances in order to see the task completed. Even my father-in-law, Mr. Horace Saunders, who came to visit my wife while she was in the hospital most of April and May, pitched in and helped us. Brother Saunders together with brother Bill Clark tore down a wall and made an arch that enabled us to join two rooms together to use as a meeting place and a fellowship hall. However, in spite of all this going on we did not totally neglect the spiritual aspect of Netivyah.

On June 3rd and 4th we had a Marriage Enrichment Seminar with Dr. Paul Faulkner and

Dr. Carl Breechen.

The Seminar is only for married couples and we had about 65 people who attended the Seminary and enjoyed every minute of it. This was the first time that we had brothers from the United States come and give us intensive teaching on any subject. We all felt that the subject of marriage was very important and pertinent to the on-growth of the believers in Israel.

For the first time we have an office in Jerusalem. We have fixed it up to be a comfortable place to work in. The most important thing is that we have a tremendous opportunity to sit, on a regular basis, with people and study the word of God without having to run around all over the country and all over Jerusalem.

The people now know where to find me and know what is going on at all times. As a result a tremendous flood of requests and appointments has overtaken us from the first day that we opened the office.

Let me share with you something about the people that we are teaching right now. Rami is an Israeli in his late 20's, brought up on a kibbutz, now serving in the police force and learning special police work in an institute in Jerusalem. The Gospel was introduced to Rami five years ago by some volunteers who had come to the kibbutz to spend their summer. Since that time

Rami has done everything possible to escape the implication of the Gospel. There were some years that he spent trying his best to ignore the deep desire in his heart to get to know Yeshua more intimately. However, a few months ago when Rami went with some friends to Eilat he met a young Dutchman who is an evangelical and who preaches to the people who sleep on the beach of the Red Sea. This young Dutchman gave Rami the name and address of a Jewish young lady in Jerusalem. When Rami contacted her and told her he wanted to learn more about the Gospel she referred Rami to me. Since that time we have been studying together, at least twice a week, very intensively and systematically. Rami wants to learn the Gospel in such a way that he will be able to teach and persuade his friends that Yeshua is truly the Messiah. Rami's original intention was to study privately especially about the accusations which the Jewish people make against the Messiah. However, our Tuesday afternoon study has turned into a class at which we had ten people this last week. People hear that I am teaching this material to Rami and they ask to come and join in. Even people from other congregations and persuasions in Jerusalem are anxious to come and study with us this subject which Rami is so interested in. So therefore, we have developed into a Monday and Tuesday afternoon class that studies the polemics which have been leveled against Christianity by the encounters of Jews and Christians throughout the last two millennia.

Mr. B.Z. is an immigrant from the United States, an Orthodox Jew, and a computer programmer. He immigrated to Israel about a year and a half ago and encountered some Jews who believed in Yeshua as the Messiah. It bothered him very much that in a Jewish state he would find such people. When he talked to them he became very interested in the New Testament and in Yeshua so he decided to study. In the beginning he was very fearful and approached us almost secretly not desiring to have fellowship with us but just to examine the subject to its depth. Now Mr. B.Z. is a regular attendant of all of our functions and is already expressing some faith in Yeshua and in the fact that Yeshua is the Messiah. The thing that seems to be threatening Mr. B.Z. most is that he would feel pressured and alienated from the Jewish community to which he feels a very strong attachment and the anti-Semitism which has been so deeply rooted in "Christendom".

In Tel Aviv our situation is quite similar. Our class has grown. We have a steady stream of new people being brought by different members of the congregation. We now number about 20 and have very intense studies every Thursday afternoon in the Gospel of Matthew. Two of the most recent additions to our group in Tel Aviv have been a couple of Jewish sisters - Israeli who hold responsible jobs in the Israeli Defense Industry.

(Originally their parents came from North Africa.) They have been extremely interested in what we are studying - especially the practical implications of the sermon on the Mount for their life in Israel today.

We want to praise the Lord together for these two sisters and for all the dozens of other people who spend hours and hours in Bible study with us every week thus preparing the way for obedience and submission totally to the King of the Jews, Yeshua from Nazareth. I could go on and on and tell you a lot of human-interest stories about the people that are participating and studying with us in Netivyah right now. However, the most exciting things are yet to come.

Sister Ahuvah Ben-Meir has gone to Finland. We both were invited to go and do some more teaching and hold special seminars about the first century church and Israel today. However, I could not go so Ahuvah went alone in order to serve as a liaison and encouragement to those people who are already in contact with us to continue in their way. She will also help with the fund raising among our friends in Finland. A h u v a has reported to me that since she arrived in Finland some $14,000 has come into our account in Finland for the building. Right now our total amount of money stands at $135,000. We have paid $100,000 already. We have $35,000 in our account and still lack $65,000 to finish the first stage of the building in Jerusalem. We are hoping to raise another $100,000 so we can build the auditorium on the roof and maybe have enough to buy off the rights of the protected tenants. However, all in all, I must say that we are absolutely surprised and absolutely astounded by the mercy and the grace of God toward us here in Netivyah. We feel, that the support which has been shown to us by people throughout the world is a clear indication that we bought this building in God's good time and with His complete backing.

Our plans for the future are varied and many. However, basically we would like to start a curriculum this fall that will present to the Israeli public and the Jewish believers in Jerusalem a total picture of the Gospel.

Including answers about who, what, and what for is the Yeshua of Nazareth. The Israeli public is ripe for a non-sectarian, non-denominational, non-churchy approach to Yeshua Mashiach. We believe that the Lord has placed us here just in the right time to see fruit forthcoming. Right now we have a couple of families who are well on the way to obedience of the Gospel. They have come to this very question. They have had some encounters with Christian circles and were quite disappointed with them in the sense that they didn't see the reason behind much of what Christians were doing in light of the New Testament. Therefore they have finally arrived at our congregation with a desire to see a New Testament, basic, and simple community.

We want to urge all of you to follow in the footsteps of people like Veiko Verho - a man whom we met a year ago in Finland. When he came to visit us here in Israel he expressed a desire to become a part of our congregation and is planning to move to Israel from Finland. He is retired and has sold one of his homes and given $40,000 to Netivyah. I know that that is an unusual case and we don't expect every one of you to go and do likewise. However, let that be an example of a person who wants to follow and be like the believers in the first century. Although we do not publish the names and amounts of what everybody gives, I did want to use Mr. Veiko Verho as an example to show you the dedication and implication that people have toward the Gospel, as it was in the first century, in countries that are hearing for the first time the Restoration plea.

Let me express to every one of you my personal gratitude and the gratitude of all the congregation in Jerusalem for your generosity and your goodness toward all of us. There have been friends in the United States who have made special contributions in their congregations and who have given far above their ability To all those we want to say - May the Lord God of Abraham bless you as He has promised to bless all those that bless Israel. Mya we all live to see the coming of the Lord in the clouds in our day.

Much love to all of you,

Joseph and Marcia Shulam

P.S.

Marcia is still ill and we are still asking all of you to pray for her health and for MR Veiko Verho's wife who has also been seriously ill with arteriosclerosis.

THE BIBLICAL GROUNDS FOR A JEWISH EXPRESSION IN THE LORD'S BODY

From Teaching from Zion , Vol 1 No 8, July 1983

Egerton Swan, in a symposium held by the Society of Jews and Christians in London, 1934, said,

> *"Judaism and Christianity are nearest to an agreement when Judaism is most unambiguously Jewish and Christianity most unambiguously Christian."*

But Jews and Christians alike have to acknowledge and even to experience in their spiritual life the immanence of Israel in Christianity. New and fruitful meeting between Judaism and Christianity implies a certain Judaization of the Christians as well as a certain completion of the Jews' Judaism. I look forward to a revival of Jewish spiritual values among Christians; and if I had to express the trend of his book in terms of the New

Testament, I would write here these two verse:

> *"...and, as his custom was, He went into*
> *the synagogue on the Sabbath day and*
> *stood up to read." (Luke 4:16), and,*

> *"they, continuing daily with one accord in*
> *the Temple, and breaking bread from house*
> *to house, did eat their meat with gladness*
> *and singleness of heart." (Acts 2:46).*

The attitude here expressed is that of Lev Gillet, a student of Oxford, and a Russian Orthodox priest, and is stated in his great book, Communion in the Messiah. However, before I even start, I would like for it to be clearly understood that I, like Paul, can say with my whole heart,

> *"whatever was to my profit I now consider*
> *loss for the sake of the Messiah. What is*
> *more, I consider everything a loss compared*
> *to the surpassing greatness of knowing the*
> *Messiah Yeshua my Lord, for whose sake I*
> *have lost all things. I consider them rubbish,*
> *that I may gain the Messiah, and be found in*
> *Him, not having a righteousness of my own*
> *that comes from the law, but that which is*
> *through faith in the Messiah." (Phil. 3:7-9)*

For this very reason it is imperative for Jews who believe that Yeshua is their Messiah and Lord, to leave the traditional, false, and antisemitic church and to return to the true New Testament church which allowed, and in fact recommended true freedom in the Messiah--freedom which makes the gospel universal--it gives the Jew the faith in the Messiah without taking away the rich heritage of God's election. And, it gives the non-Jew the freedom to be a brother and a Christian without having to become a Jew.

The Biblical base for a Jewish expression of faith: the early Jewish believers continued to be practicing Jews.

> *Acts 2:46 : "Every day they continued to meet together in the Temple courts."*

> *Acts 3:1: "One day Peter and John were going up to the Temple at the time of prayer."*

> *Acts 5:12: "The apostles performed many miraculous signs and wonders among the people. And all the believers used to meet together in Solomon's Colonnade." (If they were taught as non-Jews do you think that the people would let them meet in the Temple."*

Acts 10:13,28: "Then a voice told him, 'Get up, Peter, kill and eat'. Surely not, Lord! I have never eaten anything impure or unclean."...
"You are well aware that it is against our law for a Jew to associate with a Gentile or visit him. But God has shown me that I should not call any man impure or unclean."

Acts 15:5: "Then some of the believers who belonged to the party of the Pharisees stood up and said, 'The Gentiles must be circumcised and required to obey the law of Moses."

Acts 15:19: The words of James--"It is my judgment, therefore, that we should not make it difficult for the Gentiles who are turning to God. Instead we should write to them, telling them to abstain from pollution of idols, immorality, meat strangled, and blood."

Acts 16:1-3: Paul's circumcision of Timothy, because his mother was Jewish, was for the fact that the Jews in that area knew that his father was Gentile; it was important for Paul that Timothy be recognized as a Jew if he would travel with him . This is the reason he, himself, had Timothy circumcised.

Acts 17:2: "As his custom was, Paul went into the synagogue, and on three Sabbath days he reasoned with them from the Scriptures . "

(Cd. Beza+KJV) Acts 17:21: "But (he) bade them farewell, saying, I must by all means keep this feast that cometh in Jerusalem: but I will return."

(Acts 20: 6, 16) : "But we sailed from Philippi after the Feast of Unleavened Bread, and five days later joined the others... Paul had decided to sail past Ephesus to avoid spending time in the province of Asia, for he was in a hurry to reach Jerusalem, if possible, by the day of Pentecost."

Acts 21:20: "You see, brother, how many thousands of Jews have believed, and all of them are zealous for the law."

These Jewish believers received three false rumors about Paul's theology--that becoming believers in the Messiah necessitated:

a) To reject the laws of Moses.

b) Forbidding the circumcision of Jewish boys,

c) Being torn away from the Jewish way of life and from the traditions. A recommendation was made by the leaders of the church in Jerusalem, and among them James, that Paul address himself to this new controversy by demonstrating the falseness of the rumors against him.(Acts 21:21-24.)

> *Acts 22:3: Then Paul said: 'I am a Jew, born in Tarsus of Cilicia, but brought up in this city. Under Gamaliel I was thoroughly trained in the law of our fathers and was just as zealous for God as any of you are today..."*

> *Acts 24: 14-18: "I admit that I worship the God of our fathers, as a follower of the Way which they call a sect. I believe everything that agrees with the law and that is written in the Prophets, and I have the same hope in God as these men, that there will be a resurrection of both the righteous and the wicked. keep my conscience clear before God and man. After an absence of several years, I came to Jerusalem to bring my people gifts for the poor and to present offerings. I was ceremonially clean when they found me in the Temple courts doing t h i s . . . "*

> *Acts 25:8 : "I have done nothing wrong*

*against the law of the Jews or against
the Temple or against Caesar."*

*Acts 26:20: "First to those in Damascus,
then to those in Jerusalem and in all Judea,
and to the Gentiles also, I preached that
they should repent and turn to God and
prove their repentance by their deeds."*

It is clear from Paul's own life that he does not teach the Jews to leave their heritage in the law. In fact he, himself, gives witness that he kept the law, and the feasts, and even purification rituals in the Temple. The church in Jerusalem had many Jews, and they were all zealous to the law. No one condemned them, no one saw in them a heretical sect.

We can therefore conclude by stating:

a) The New Testament does not forbid the Jew who believes in Yeshua as the Messiah and Lord to live like a Jew and to observe whatever Jewish customs he might wish.

b) The keeping of Jewish customs does not necessitate a rejection of the Grace of God, and the being under the law. (In other words, you can be a good Jew and a good faithful Christian at the same time.)

The big problem is not keeping the law, but the

judgment of others when they either keep the law for the wrong reason--namely, atonement, salvation, meritoriously, or with pride over their Gentile brethren, or when there are Jews who forced the Gentiles to keep the Jewish laws, and by so doing annulled the Grace and freedom we have in the Messiah.

We realize that there are many difficult questions and pit-falls in the approach of Restoration Christianity--it is not easy to restore the freedom that we have as redeemed in the Blood of the Messiah. It is also not easy to re-establish the Jewish expression of Messianic faith as it was in the first century. But, I believe that the Messianic Synagogues that have come up throughout the world, and are re-evaluating their position in light of the New Testament text, will be a vibrant, true Body of the Lord-- and will live side-by-side with the whole church of Christ. Just as there are Mexican churches, and Vietnamese churches, and Polish, Russian, and Chinese churches, and all of these are a part of the Body of the Lord, so, there will be a Jewish expression of the children of the Jewish Messiah that saved the whole human race on the Cross.

The Methodological aspect . The Fuller methods of evangelism have spread through the Evangelical world like wildfire. In reality there is nothing new in what they call "Cross cultural communication." The Apostle Paul already early in his ministry states:

> *"Though I am free and belong to no man, I*
> *make myself a slave to everyone, to win as*
> *many as possible. under the law I became*
> *like one under the law (though I myself am*
> *not under the law), so as to win those under*
> *the law.   God's law, but am under*
> *the law of the Messiah.)... I have become*
> *all things to all men so that by all possible*
> *means I might save some." (I Cor. 9:19-22)*

If this was good enough for Paul--why, pray I, should it not be good enough for us here in Israel, the very place where the call came to Peter to go and teach the Gentiles, ought to be the place where we should proclaim freedom to the Jew to remain a good Jew, but to find his saving grace in Yeshua, his Messiah, Son of the Living God.

When in 1975 Mr. R.T. Coote, wrote his article, "How Kosher Can Christianity Get?" There were in the USA only six so-called Messianic Synagogues, and only about 300 people who attended these Synagogues. Today, there are 46 congregations which call themselves "Messianic" and close to 5,000 people who attend them regularly. Well over 100% growth; in some places like Philadelphia, PA they started with 16 people and now they number well over 200 people. Similar growth has been experienced in no "Christian denomination", and we must say that God has blessed, even if the whole movement has not yet dealt with the totality of the theological and practical problems that still face it.

We hope that all of Christianity will continue to search for its roots, and for the full and perfect will of the Lord--in order to draw closer and closer to God. We must not be satisfied with the traditions of the divided and apostate historical church. We must rise above the tradition and return back to the clear expression of God's will and attitudes. I believe that it can be done, and that we have more tools today than people like Augustine or Aquinas had in their days. Let us get up and rise to the task with fresh strength supplied from the Holy Spirit and the Word of God. As the day and the hour of Israel's Salvation comes near we will see more and more Jews receive Yeshua as their personal Messiah, the Son of God. Let those who are in the wrong and who are still motivated by the traditional anti-Jewish feelings of the historical church come out from among her and stand by the throng on Mount Zion to sing praises to the Son of David. We can do this together, Jews and Gentiles, with respect for each other and with the freedom that we afford in the Messiah our Lord. Let all Christians who are truth seekers stand up and be counted with obedience to our King, honor and dignity to all men, and shame to none. May the

Lord be glorified in our lives and may we walk in the unity of His Spirit.

MAY GOD IN HIS KINDNESS HAVE MERCY ON US

From Teaching from Zion , Vol 1 No 8, July 1983

Elie Wiesel in his book, **The Oath**, has a very perplexing passage. Moshe the son of the tailor was speaking at the synagogue on Saturday morning. These are the words which Moshe spoke to the worthy assembly: You are forcing me to speak, very well... Because I have eyes to see, you fear me. Because I see through your veils, you feel threatened and draw closer to one another. Yet God sees better and further and more clearly than I - and Him you do not fear? May He in His Kindness have mercy on you. You do not deserve His love, only His compassion! The congregants bowed their heads as one. The Rebbe nodded his approval - he always agreed with visiting preachers.

I do not know of any of my preacher friends who would have not liked to speak those same words on a thousand occasions. The truth of this statement reverberates through the hallmark of prophetic utterances. As a Jew who believes that Yeshua, Son of David, is the Messiah, I sometimes feel the strong urge to get up in the synagogue and feel forced to speak as this Moshe did in Wiesel's novel. However, other times I feel that the same words might fit better in many churches.

We are plagued with the syndrome of consensus - all of us must fit the mold fashioned by the footsteps of those who have gone before us in the wrong paths. We have taken a vow of silence - a conspiracy to be polite and always hold our cue - never, never to say anything which might be considered impertinent. A vow such as this could not have been taken by Jeremiah, Amos, or Peter. They would have rebelled against the norm set by men of the cloth and taken sides in the camp of the lone prophet, then crowned King, Yeshua.

The mark of the early church was in the willingness of the Christians to give up their social, political, and economic status, even their lives, for the sake of the truth. They feared God first and said "yes" to Him and "no" to men. We fear men and say "yes" to them and "no" to God.

The prophet Isaiah said:

> *"For the Lord spoke to me with a strong hand, and instructed me that I should not walk in the way of these people...sanctify the Lord of Hosts himself; and let Him be your fear, and let Him be your dread." (Isaiah 8:10-13)*

This issue does not only apply to the Jewish people who if they would be afraid of God more and less of the rabbis would have long ago accepted Yeshua as the Messiah. However, Christians in the 20th century are not exempt from the same reprimand. One could say to us today what Yeshua said to the Pharisees in His day:

> *"The Scribes and Pharisees sit in Moses' seat : All therefore whatsoever they bid you observe,...but do not yet after their words for they say and do not".*

My dear friends and brothers with the resources which God has put in our hands we could bring the world, or at least most of it, right to its knees. Our experience in "Netivyah" has brought us a sense of awe for the power of God and what Christians can do when they really believe in something.

We have received almost $100,000 in the course of six weeks. Much of this money came from people who do not live in the U.S.A. and from whom we didn't expect to receive anything. We worried and stewed over how we would get such large amounts of money. We feared men and God showed us that there is nothing to fear from men if we fear Him. I call both Jews and Christians to fear God, talk less, and do more.

THE ELECTIVE IMPERATIVE - BETWEEN I WANT AND I HAVE TO

From Teaching from Zion , Vol 1 No 8, July 1983

The International Wildlife Association has made the preservation of extinct animals a world issue. Time, Newsweek, and every major newspaper has ads and articles with the panda bear preaching the gospel of preservation for such mammoths as whales and polar bears.

I would like to call to your attention a very near and dying breed of creature - the "duty called person". A man who knows that there are things which must be accomplished, tasks awaiting completion and "the buck stops here" is becoming an extinct creature. The above statement might be a generalization and might not be true in every case. However, we know from the apostle Paul that he felt a debt to mankind - a duty which had to be paid - a task which had to be accomplished.

However, if the idea is true to any degree, then the theology of grace has swung the pendulum too far to the right. People have heard for so much of their church life sermons about grace and how they are not saved through law. They have forgotten that it is not those who say "Lord, Lord" who will inherit the Kingdom of Heaven. In the Restoration Movement we have preached that not the hearer of the Word but the doer of it will be saved. These important personal and corporate responsibilities exhaust the repertoire of "have to's" in the 20th century church which wants to be like the 1st century Christians.

I write these things not in order to push against the grace of God through Yeshua our Messiah but in order to remind us as those under grace that there is more to being a Christian than "Religious" things. Let me use an exegesis of a famous passage of scripture to illustrate my point: I Cor. 10:1-22.

Paul's first point (vs. 1-4) is that the Exodus experience was a prototype of salvation to the children of Israel. In other words, we like them and they like us have established a relationship with the Messiah by the same means.

We are baptized - they were baptized in the crossing of the Sea leaving their enemy to drown in the Sea of Death. We receive the Holy Spirit in baptism - they also received it in the cloud. We eat with the Lord on His table - they also ate with the

Lord and even drank from Him, our Rock.

However, Paul's point in verse 5 is that baptism and eating with the Lord is not enough to be assured of salvation. If I put this point in modern terms, Paul is telling these early disciples that it was simply not enough to be baptized and to eat at the Lord's table - these are the minimum. Verse 6 comes out and states it directly - "these things are a warning for us, not to desire evil as they did".

In the history of Israel there is no generation which has received greater grace from God than in the wilderness. This generation is described by Jeremiah, the prophet, in these words:

> *"I remember thee ,the kindness of thy youth,*
> *the love of thine betrothal when you followed*
> *after me in the wilderness..." (Jer. 2:2)*

In the wilderness God revealed Himself to Israel in such a dramatic way. He led them day by day and every night by the presence of the cloud and the pillar of fire. Oh, how I wish that every day I would know for sure where God wants me - like my forefathers knew in the wilderness.

These wandering nomadic tribes of Hebrews had the privilege of building the tent of meeting for the Lord's presence in the midst of the camp. They had Moses as their leader. Moses was a leader who was willing for God to blot him out of His book for the sake of Israel. Yet in spite of all these blessings Paul states that God was not pleased with that generation. I truly wonder sometimes if God is pleased with our generation of Christians - yes, even with those who go to church regularly, break bread, etc.

The New Testament does not keep us in the dark. It tells us why God was displeased with the Israelites in the wilderness. Verse 7:

> *"do not be idolaters . . . . a s it is*
> *written, 'the people sat down to eat*
> *and drink and rose up to dance "*

In verse 8 immorality is stated in reference to the marriage of the Midianites and the advice which Balaam gave them. In verse 9, they put the Lord to the test, tempted the Lord and were destroyed by serpents.

In verse 13 Paul states for the Christians of the first century that no temptation has overtaken them which is not common to men. This statement is put here in order to counter the excuse commonly heard: "Well, if I had lived then it wouldn't happen to me." Let us, my dear brothers in Christ, remember that God with all His love and grace did not spare the generation of the wilderness because of idolatry, immorality, and a religion of tempting God and being ungrateful.

We, ourselves, keep the religious things but do we keep those commandments which Yeshua (Jesus in Hebrew) turn the other cheek, give to him who asks you, refuse not to him who would borrow from you, when you give alms, sound no trumpet before y o u . . . . , in praying do not heap empty phrases....

One rabbi told me: "The Christians believe in Jesus but it would be good for all if they would believe Jesus." There is no doubt that we are all short of God's perfection. However, that is no excuse for not hearing and doing what Yeshua commanded. Let us try to overcome the church bench religion. Let our light shine and our world change. It is not enough to be "born again" - we must live again.

THE LAUSANNE COMMITTEE TASK-FORCE FOR JEWISH EVANGELISM

From Teaching from Zion, Vol 1 No. 9, November 1983

A group of fifty-two delegates, from ten countries on five continents, met for a consultation at Newmarket, England, from 29 August, 1983 to 2 September, 1983. The purpose was to engage in Biblical study and discussion of topical theological and missiological issues relating to Jewish evangelism. I participated in the name of "Netivyah" as a delegate in this Newmarket consultation.

The outcome of the consultation was far beyond my expectations. I really expected to be with a bunch of denominational clergy who would sit drinking tea and talking about Jewish evangelism as if it were a safari. This is, at least, the picture I had of all those British heads of missionary associations. To be honest with you, some of them filled the bill. However, in general, I must say that I found people who had a genuine interest in teaching Jewish people about the Messiah and people who were open to learn and disagree with one another in love. The subjects which were focused upon were:

> Theological and Sociological Concerns of Jewish Believers in Jesus;

> The Theological Significance of Israel; and Christian Witness to the Jewish People Today.

There were some statements which expressed the general consensus of the subjects under discussion. Although, on some of the issues I would have liked to have seen a much stronger, or more Biblical, attitude expressed. The outcome, in general, was satisfactory when you consider the far distance which the delegates transverse.

HERE ARE A FEW OF THE STATEMENTS MADE:

•We appeal to our fellow Christians to recognize that Jewish believers have the freedom to keep or not to keep certain customs and practices that are prescribed in the Mosaic Law, while continuing to rely solely upon the sufficiency of Christ for salvation. The Law which was given by God through Moses is part of the heritage of both Jews and Christians.

•We affirm that God has not cast away His people.

We call upon all Christians to pray that the Jewish people may be saved. Furthermore, we call upon all Christians to acknowledge the continued election of the people of Israel, and their return to the Land of the Fathers as evidence of God's faithfulness.

There were some statements which were not accepted by the majority but they were things which the group reflected upon. One of these was a statement about the attitude that Christians should have toward Rabbinic Judaism.

• "We recognize that rabbinic Judaism has rejected Jesus as the Messiah and the New Testament as Scriptures. However, this rejection of our faith and the basis of our faith does not mean that rabbinic Judaism is irrelevant to us and has nothing from which we may learn. Throughout the centuries, rabbinic Judaism kept the Jewish people together and gave them identity as a chosen people. It has developed and still lives out a core of a Biblical heritage which was largely forgotten by the Gentile church, and Gentile believers may learn from Jewish tradition in areas of ethics, communal and family life, Biblical festivals, and in terms of corporate historical identity. Whereas this learning process will help the believer to understand his own Biblical roots and see more of the inside of Jewish life and identity, it would naturally lead to a greater concern for the Jewish people and to a desire to witness to them the living Messiah."

A very important statement was also made by Dr. Gerald Anderson who is the editor of "International Bulletin of Missionary Research" one of the more prestigious papers on missiological subjects. Dr. Anderson said:

> *"The Christian conviction that Jesus Christ is for everyone is so fundamental and pervasive in the New Testament that to believe and maintain otherwise requires one either to ignore the New Testament, or to do surgery on it and eliminate the substance of the truth, or to engage in revisionist and speculative interpretation of Scripture."*

All three of these approaches have been advocated and employed by those scholars who maintain today that the Church has no missionary obligation to the Jews; that the Jewish people have their own covenant which is sufficient for salvation and do not need the Gospel of Jesus Christ; and that therefore the mission of the Church does not pertain to the Jews.

It is my judgment and concern that if the Jewish people, who were the original focus of Jesus mission, do not need Christ, then a similar theological case can be projected (as some are already doing) to apply to others. The mission to the Jews is where the Christian mission began. In fact it can be argued that the mission was initially understood as only to the Jews, and later as 'to the Jew first'.

It is indeed ironic that whereas in the primitive church the two most fundamental controversies were whether the Gospel was for anyone other than the Jews, and then whether Gentiles had to become Jews in order to be Christians. Today, the controversies involve the issues of whether the Gospel is intended to include Jews and then whether Jews have to become Gentiles in order to be Christians.

In summary, the mission to Jews is the keystone of the Christian mission to all the peoples of the world - to the whole creation - and if this keystone is removed, the universal mission of the Church is in danger of theological collapse.

Quite clearly, there is no exemption of the Jews from the universal Christian mission. My theological point is that either all people need Christ or none do! This affirmation of the Lordship of Jesus Christ is inherent and fundamental in the New Testament and in historical Christian faith."

Evangelicals would agree that "a church without a message for the Jews lacks one for the Gentiles as well" (Jacob Jocz, cited by J. Verkuyl, Contemporary Missiology, page 136). As Johannes Verkuyl has rightly observed, "To be willing to speak about

the Gospel to all people except the Jews would be
nothing less than spiritual antisemitism".

The importance of Dr. Anderson's statement is
that a main line evangelical has declared the
importance of the Gospel for the Jewish people and
the interdependent relationship of Israel and the
"Church". The realization that God has made the
destiny of Israel and the "Church" so interwoven
and dependent on one another that to separate
these two might mean the end of the "Church".
If I would use Pauline terms it would mean that
the branches of the wild olive tree would cut
themselves off the root. "Christians" cannot shake
off the responsibility to Israel and the Jewish
people. They must face both the gruesome past
and the glorious future that God has prepared for
both. In the first century Paul did all things to
see Israel's destiny fulfilled by the preaching of
the Gospel to the Jews. He collected funds from
the Gentile Christians to help the poor saints in
Judea. Paul even did this with the full knowledge
that he might be imprisoned when he arrived in
Jerusalem. He thought that Jews must know that
through the blood of the Messiah the Gentiles are
fulfilled into the covenant with the God of Israel.

For those who would want to be like the
first century Church, it would be good to not
only develop a framework of the early church's
practices but also an attitude of the early church
toward the Jews and Israel.   We hope that

"Netivyah" can help you to see your place within God's purpose in a much clearer light. If you're a Jew, see what God has done through Yeshua by you for the world. If you are a Gentile, see what God has done for you through Israel's Messiah, Yeshua. We want to bless you for your help to "Netivyah" and hope that the Lord will bless you so that you can help also in the future. We need to finish the full purchase of the property and enlarge our tents. We need your help!!!

MAY THE LORD BLESS YOU AND KEEP YOU AND MAKE HIS FACE TO SHINE UPON YOU AND GIVE YOU PEACE.

THE IMAGE OF YESHUA THE TALMUD

From Teaching from Zion, Vol 1 No. 9, November 1983

During the long years of exile in Christian countries the Jew was forced to hide the literature by which he governed his life - the tradition of the Rabbis which was recorded in the Jerusalem and Babylonian Talmuds. The reason for this fear was imbedded in a strong anti-Christian and anti-Jesus tradition which is found in Fear, hate, and prejudice through the centuries has blinded both sides from discovery and retroversion of important and valuable facts about the relationship and the character of Yeshua and his disciples. What we now want is to glean some of these facts which would help us. However, at times, it would be necessary to peel off encrusted coats of tradition which has been garaged there by the misfortune of Jewish-Christian controversy.

I.   The Birth of Yeshua

The Talmudic sources cannot make up their mind either on <u>time</u> or his <u>father's</u> name, nor the <u>mother.</u>

a) <u>The Time</u>

1.The Story in Sotah 47a states that Yeshua lived in the days of Yehoshua ben Perachya who lived in the 2nd century before Yeshua Ha-Mashiach.

2. In B. Hagiaga 4b it is stated that Yeshua lived in the time of Rabbi Akiva, that is in the first years of t h e 2nd century A.D. (See also Berakhot 61b.) In the same tradition which is in Hagiga 4 it is implied that He and his mother, Miryam the hairdresser, lived in the days of Rav Bibi who is a 4th century A.D. Amora.

We see that even though we have only brought the statements made in the Talmud about the time and birth of. Yeshua, it is abundantly clear that the Talmud does not have a clear tradition preserved as to the birth. However, in later periods Jewish scholars who saw the contradictions wrote: "for this story as to Miryam, the women's hairdresser, mother of Jesus." (Tosafot Hagiga 4b)

b) <u>Father's Name</u>

1. Gittin 90a states that the husband of

Yeshua's mother was called Paphos Ben-Yehudah who, by the way, lived in the time of Rabbi Akiva, who lived in the first part of the 2nd century. 67a states that Yeshua was called the Son of Stada, who was hanged in Lod on the day before Passover. Shabbat 104b has the same information but attempts to connect it with the tradition of Yehoshua Ben-Perachya's coming back from Egypt. This is a story of the 2nd century BCE.

2.   In Sanhedrin 67a we find another tradition as to the father of Yeshua - that his name was not Ben-Stada but Ben-Pandera. In fact, right in that place we see that these two traditions clash and produce in the late period of the Amoraim an attempt to harmonize. "Rav Chida said: "Ben-Stada is Ben-Pandera, the husband of Stada is Paphos Ben Yeshua, Pandera is her paramour. Is it not that his mother is Miryam the women's hairdresser! As they say in Pumbedita she is Sata-da from her husband."

In addition to the fact that the Talmud is mixed up in regard to the parents of Yeshua and his name, we see that the largest portion of material which is historical in character recognizes that his name is Yeshua of

Nazareth. (Avodah Zarah 16b-17a.)

" I was once walking in the upper street of Sepphoris; there by the name of Jacob of K'far S'khanya...." Also in the Sanhedrin 43a.

From these stories we see that the collections of contradictory material about Yeshua in the Talmud could not pass undetected even before the end of the time of the Amoraim. (5th century C.E.) Rav Chisda, in the third generation of Babylonian Rabbis, attempts to harmonize the different views by changing the name Stada, which appears as the name of Yeshua's father in the earlier material, to the name of the mother because it has similar intonation to Sotah - which in Aramaic means "unfaithful" and by giving the record of this Midrash on the same name in Pumbedita. Pumbedita was the big Jewish center in Babylon during the 5th century. In this Babylonian center they could not understand the contradictions in the material handed down to them and attempted to harmonize it by changing the name of the father to that of the mother of Yeshua. From this we can see that most of this negative, slanderous material was fabricated.

It is clear from a socio-psychological view that such slanderous material was commonly applied to anyone who was the object of hate.

In fact, from Tacitus one can learn that many of the accusations against Yeshua in Judaism were earlier attributed to Moses by the Roman and Greek historians.

"Moses, in order to make his hold on the people stronger founded new laws - laws which are against those of most other peoples and human beings.... That which was not allowed in our eyes, he, Moses made it allowed and pure in their eyes.... The image of the animal which is most despised in our eyes he put in the Holy of Holies as a sacrifice to God.... There are those who say that they (the Jews) started by resting and doing nothing on the Sabbath day. This the Jews do because their heart is after sloth, laziness, and They have taken this attitude to the point that every seventh year they do nothing... The rest of Evil and Bad law...."

We see from this quotation in Tacitus that slander and evil propaganda often take the same lines of thought. Some of the same slander that is brought against Yeshua was directly taken from things which were earlier said about Moses by different pagan anti-Jewish polemicists.

II. The Teaching of Yeshua As Reflected In the Talmud

When we look at this material we must remember that from the beginning, its object was not to report what Yeshua taught or how the early church viewed the teaching which they received from the apostles. So we need to read between the lines in order to see what we can learn about the teaching of Yeshua.

Let us first look at the story reported in Avodah Zarah 16b-17a and Tosefta Chullin II, 24.

"Our rabbis teach: When R. Eliezer was arrested for minut,("heresy, infidelity, suspicion of being a Jewish Christian"') they brought him up to the tribunal for judgment. The court said to him, 'Does an elder such as you occupy himself with such useless matters?' He answered 'I rely on the Judge.' The judge of the court thought he said it concerning him, whereas he said it with reference to his Father who is in Heaven. He, the court, said to him: 'Since you have faith in me - dismissed - you are released.'

When he returned home his disciples came into comfort him but he would not accept their solace. R. Akiva said to him, Rabbi, will you permit me to say a word of what you have taught me? He replied, Say. Said he to him, Rabbi, perhaps minut has come to hand and has pleased you and on account of that you

were arrested. He replied: 'Akiva, you reminded
me!' Once I was walking on the upper street
of Sepphoris and found one of the disciples of
Yeshua the Nazarite by the name of Jacob, a
man from K'far S'Khanya. He said to me, It is
written in your Torah: 'Thou shalt not bring
the hire of a harlot, etc.' How about making
it a privy for the high priest? But I could not
answer him at all. He told me, 'Thus did Yeshua
the Nazarene teach me: 'For the hire of a harlot
hath she gathered them and unto the hire of
a harlot shall they return; from the place of
filth they came, and unto the place of filth
they go.' And the utterance pleased me. On
account of this I was arrested for minut....."

The same story appears in Tosefta Chullin II, 24 with minor differences. Rabbi Eliezer Ben-Hyrcanus was a disciple of Yochanan Ben-Zakkai, who was one of the most important rabbis during the destruction of the Joseph Klausner dates the story about 110 CE. There are some whose date for this 66-68 CE, which would make it possible in their view to say that Jacob of K'far S'Khanya is none other than Jacob (James), the brother of Yeshua.

From the point of view of teaching, in this case, Yeshua is reported to give a simple solution to a real halakhic problem. But the solution itself and the way in which it was learned, namely through a verse from the prophet Micah 1:7, is the uniqueness of Yeshua's teaching which could make a person like Rabbi Eliezer astounded.

It is clear that these stories in the Babylonian Talmud had nothing to do with the truth which the New Testament accurately records. These are stories which circulated among the Babylonian rabbis in the 3rd to 5th century after Yeshua. However, there are important things to learn from these stories, because they do express the feelings of Jews in ancient times. Here are two points which can be learned from the Talmud about the Jewish attitude to Yeshua:

a) The Rabbis did not have a clear tradition about the Father of Yeshua. If they had had one, don't you think they would have taught it.

b) The Rabbis were impressed with the teaching of Yeshua even to the point that some actually were brought to the Roman court for their faith and were accused for minut. You must remember t h a t the Rabbis thought that they had an exclusive right to interpret the Law. When Rabbi Eliezer is thought to have been impressed by the teaching of Yeshua as reported by Jacob of Sikhania, this is no light matter for the Talmud to report . The Talmud could have just not reported this event, like many others which they killed by silence. The reason they chose, in this case, to report the story was to show the greatness of Rabbi Akiva. The same Akiva that misled the nation of Israel to follow Bar-Kochba, the false messiah. This story was saved only for the sake of Rabbi Akiva. We have in it an important teaching about the relationship of Jews and Jewish believers in Yeshua in the beginning of the second century.

In this next issue of Teaching from Zion, we will deal with more stories which are in the Talmud about Yeshua. These things are important even just for the general education of the believer, who ought to know that they exist and to learn how to answer those who might ask him. They are also important for the picture that they paint of the different reality in the relationship of Jews and "Christians".

THE IMAGE OF YESHUA IN THE TALMUD SECTION II (CONTINUATION)

From Teaching from Zion, Vol 1, No 10, March 1984

In the last Teaching From Zion we examined the nature of the criticism on the parents of Yeshua and the circumstances of His birth. We also touched upon the attitude of the rabbis toward Yeshua's teaching from a legal point of view. In this issue, we will look at a passage which will give us insight into the views of the rabbis, their attitudes and explanations toward the teaching in Judaism that Yeshua was a heretic and an apostate. that we will deal with is probably the most famous story that rabbinical Jews believe about Yeshua. The rabbis use this story to give justification to the Jewish opposition to the Gospel and more specifically to Yeshua as a teacher of the Law. We will deal with this story and hopefully we will be able to prove that it was fabricated propaganda type story that was used as a standard procedure by the rabbis to discredit their This story, about the work of Yeshua, appears ni two major passages in Talmudic literature: Sanhedrin 107b, Sota 47a, and Haggiga 22.

I will be quoting an English translation of the story from Sanhedrin 107b.

"The Rabbis have taught: The left always be repelled, and the right on the other hand drawn nearer. But one should not do it...as R. Joshua ben P'rachyah, who thrust forth Jesus with both hands. What was the matter with regard to R. Joshua ben Prachyah? When King Jannai directed the destruction of the Rabbis, R. Joshua ben P'rachyah and Jesus went to When security returned, Rabbi Simeon ben Shetach sent him a letter to this effect: 'From me ,Jerusalem the holy city, to thee, Alexandria in Egypt, My spouse tarries in thee, and I dwell with my sister. Thereupon Joshua arose and came; and a certain inn was in his way, in which they treated him with great respect. Then spake Joshua: 'How fair is this inn (Akhsanga)!' Jesus saith to him: 'But, Rabbi, (Akhsanga-a hostess) has little narrow eyes.' Joshua replied: 'Thou godless fellow, doest thou occupy thyself things?' He directed that 400

horns should be brought, and put Him under excommunication. Jesus oftentimes came and said to him, 'Take me back.' Joshua did not trouble himself One day, just as Joshua was reading the sh'ma' (the words: 'Hear, O Israel,' Deut. VI:4 etc.), Jesus came to him, hoping that he would take Him back. Joshua made a sign to Him with his hand. Then Jesus thought that he had altogether repulsed Him, and went away, set up a brickbat, and worshiped it. Joshua said to Him: 'Be converted!' Jesus saith: 'Thus have I been taught by thee: from him that sinneth and that maketh the people to sin, is taken away the possibility of repentance.' And the Teacher [i.e. who is everywhere mentioned by this title in the Talmud] has said: 'Jesus had practiced sorcery and had corrupted and misled Israel.!"

In the second version, in the Babylonian Talmud Sotah 47a, basically the same story is brought - although it is a little shorter version. The interesting thing is that the name of Yeshua is not mentioned at all. Still, a third much shorter version, in the Jerusalem Talmud 77d we find the same basic without the mention of Yeshua and without the name of Rabbi Joshua ben P'rachyah. In place of his name, however, it has the name of his contemporary - Jehudah ben Tabbai. In other words, in these three versions we have - the Babylonian Talmud, the latest

Talmud, which mentions Yeshua as that disciple of Rabbi Joshua ben P'rachyah who went astray. The second version, also in the Babylonia Sota 47, Joshua ben P'rachyah is still mentioned but Yeshua HaMassiach is not mentioned. In the third version, the oldest version of them all, the Jerusalem Talmud we find neither Yeshua nor Joshua ben P'rachyah but Jehudah ben Tabbia. Both ben P'rachyah and ben Tabbai these men lived at the end of the second century B.C. and the beginning of the first century B.C., i.e. About a 100 years, at least, before Yeshua was born and raised in the Land of Israel.

If any of this would be true, of course, it would make our Yeshua the Messiah live at least 87 years before the historical Yeshua of the New Testament was born. presents a great historical difficulty within the Talmud itself. In the Talmud you have Yeshua living at the time of Rabbi Akiva and which means at the beginning of the second century A.D. One cannot have Yeshua living, according to the Talmud itself , from the second century B.C. to the second century A.D. - a span of over 200 years. This is absolutely clear from the story in the Talmud about Rabbi Akiva and his friends sitting in the marketplace of Sepphoris and arguing about the young man that they saw walking down the street that was supposed to be Yeshua the bastard. The reference in the Talmud for this story is Kallah 18b or in Venezia 41c edition of the Kallah. Either way you can see that there is no historical possibility, even from within the Talmudic references, for any of these stories to have historical significance. The Talmud knows that Yeshua did not live over 200 years from the days of Joshua ben Prachya to the days of Rabbi Akiva but it ignored the facts. This is true especially when you have three different versions - the oldest of which, the Jerusalem Talmud, doesn't even have the name of Yeshua associated with the story.

What really happened here? The answer to this question we can obtain from the correct explanation of a striking anachronism which the account in the Babylonian Talmud contains. The story of why Joshua ben P'rachyah escaped to Alexandra is related to Jannai who lived from 104 B.C. to 78 B.C. at about the year of 87 crucifixion of 80 Pharisees took place after the capture of the stronghold of Bethome (see Schurer's History of the Jewish People in the time of Jesus Vol. 1, page 303).

This historical event was the occasion of the flight by the Pharisees generally from Israel into Syria and them was Joshua ben P'rachyah and Jehudah ben Tabbai who fled into Alexandria. In as much as the narrative bears upon its face the stamp of a genuine account which has been disseminated in a disfigured (and for that very reason) and in many respects obscure shape, it is unquestionable that the name Yeshua is here spurious. Even if it were found in all the sources of our information, it would have been attributed to a polemic insertion of the later rabbis for the ridicule and discredit of the "Christian" faith.

However, as the case stands now the Jerusalem Talmud, i.e. the oldest version, as already mentioned does not have Yeshua's name. This very circumstance, especially in the view of the character of this Talmud, supports our decision that the name of Yeshua was originally wanting and the anachronism was first created in Babylon for the polemics of the Talmud against the rising strength of the faith in Yeshua as the Messiah. The rabbis had some valid explanation why the Jewish people ought not to believe in Yeshua. Of course, "He was truly a great student but He went sour and rebelled against His rabbi". This is the source; according to the Rabbis, of His wisdom, His knowledge of the Torah, His importance and also His apostasy.

However, as the records stand before us today from both Talmuds, we see that these stories just don't fit together. It is clear that in the Babylonian Talmud and the Sanhedrin Tractate that the name of Yeshua was inserted and used for these polemic purposes against Christians.

Why was this particular story, chosen by the Rabbis, attributed to Yeshua Son of David. First, because we have a strong tradition in the Gospel of Matthew that teaches us that Yeshua did run away with His parents, as a child, from Israel to Egypt because there was persecution here in Bethlehem. Second, the text of the New Testament does quote Hosea 1 which states "and out of Egypt I called My Son". Third, the rabbis wanted to show how serious it was for those who followed Yeshua as the Messiah and that there was no way back to repentance if they decided to come back into the fold of rabbinical Judaism. Of course, as I have mentioned earlier, the story is only attributed to Yeshua very late in the Byzantine Period in Babylon. Originally, the story had nothing to do with Jesus. Probably it had some historical grounds since it was connected to events in the days of the killing of the Pharisees and the escape of the important rabbis to Syria and Egypt. Only later was this story attributed to Yeshua out of polemics against Byzantine type "Christianity" and its attitudes toward Judaism.

Joseph Klauzner in his famous book Jesus of Nazareth states this about the above story of Yeshua:

·We have three versions of the same story. In the oldest version, found in the Jerusalem Talmud, Haggiga 22, there is no mention of the name of Yeshua at all. The whole story is attributed to Jehudah ben Tabbai and one of his addition of the name of Yeshua was in the late Babylonian version and was probably added in in connection with the name Elisha and Gehazi and with the intention of a play-on-words between Yeshu and Joshua ben P'rachyah.

•What we have here in the Babylonian version, that includes the name of Yeshua, are two "Christian" traditions about Yeshua that are found in the Gospels.

> 1) Yeshua runs away with His father to Egypt because of the persecution of Herod and

> 2) Yeshua is associated with unfaithful sinful women.

Klauzner continues and says, "the story in its form in the Babylonian Talmud is so strange and so late that it is a pity to lose any words in order to prove its falseness. Yeshua as one who bows down and worships a brick - could there be any greater absurdity than this? Yeshua was a disciple of Joshua ben P'rachyah from the generation of Shimon ben Shetach, Jannai the King from the second and first century B.C., 8 years before His birth? There is no greater historical inconsistency than this." These were the words of Joseph Klauzner - one of the most respected Jewish scholars in our century.

YESHUA, THE KING OF KINGS

From Teaching from Zion, Vol. 1, No. 11, October 1984

In this article I want us to trace out the idea of **Kingship.** I believe that this subject is essential for our understanding of the Messiahship . Why do you think that the writer of the Gospel of Matthew by the inspiration of the word of the Holy Spirit, states in Matthew 1:1 "the book of the genealogy (events) of Yeshua HaMashiach, the son of David, the son of Abraham." What was the importance of including David and Abraham in this verse?

In order to understand the Messiahship, the Kingship, we must first look at the very legal and essential aspects in these two men, David and Abraham, that makes this relationship necessary if Yeshua of Nazareth was to be truly recognized as Ha-Mashiach (the Christ). In Genesis 15:6 God gave a promise and made a covenant with Abraham that through his seed all the nations of the world would be blessed.

This covenant with Abraham stands as a pivotal point in human history. It was a covenant for the redemption of mankind through one who would be of the seed of Abraham.

The first place that kingship is mentioned as a divine institution, God ordained, is in Deuteronomy 17:13 & how God brings this subject about.

> *"When you enter the land which the Lord your God gives you, and you possess it and live in it, and you say, set a king over me like all the nations who are around me."*

What causes this anointing of the king? "We want a king like all the other nations."

The idea of a flesh and blood king in Israel was not innately a divine will of God. God didn't intend, from the beginning, for Israel to have a flesh and blood king but He gave into their desires. He allowed them to fall into the trap of a flesh and blood king. The history of Israel has proven that the institution of an earthly kingship brought our ruin. These kings brought about our destruction because of their disobedience to the Lord and their misuse of the people. As result of their disobedience we were sent into exile and Jerusalem fell - both the first and second times.

Although the people of Israel had been ruled by

judges for a period of time, they came to Samuel asking him to put a king on them "because he had grown old and his sons did not walk in his ways but turned aside after dishonest gain and took bribes and perverted justice." They wanted a king to judge them like all the nations.

Finally, in I Samuel 8:5-18 God tells Samuel that if the people want a king - give them a king but these are the laws by which this king is to be anointed by and the laws by which he is supposed to follow.

The Law had foretold that this event would happen. In verse 7 we read,

> *"the Lord said to Samuel, 'listen to the voice of the people in regard to all that they say to you, for they have not rejected you, rejected Me from being a king over them.'"*

Their desire for a flesh and blood king was a rejection of the dominion of the ruling of the Kingship of God.

So they finally had their kings - King Saul and after him King David. In the case of David, God does something that He hadn't done previously. Because of David's unique character, his repentance, and his desire to build a house for the Lord, God promises David that he would establish his throne forever. In II Samuel 7:13-16 we read,

"He shall build a house for My name, and I will establish the throne of his kingdom forever. I will be a Father to him and he will be a son to Me; when he commits iniquity, I will correct him with the rod of men and the strokes of the sons of men, but My lovingkindness shall not depart from him, as I took it away from Saul, whom I removed from before you. And your house and your kingdom shall endure before Me forever; your throne shall be established forever."

The people of Israel knew these promises that God had promised to King David. They expected these promises to be fulfilled. Yet what happened? Time after time most of the kings of Israel and Judah walked in the ways of Rehoboam and did evil in the sight of the Lord and displeased God. This was the epitaph of most of the kings of Israel and Judah.

At the end of the book of Kings, the threat of exile is repeated. Because of what the kings had or hadn't done. God was going to cast the people into exile. It came about that Jerusalem fell in the 6th century B.C. and the people, the leadership - the royal house, the priesthood, all the elect of the people found themselves in Babylon. There was no king in Judah or in Israel. A Babylonian governor was appointed to the land. Ezra and Nehemiah returned 70 years later and reestablished the temple worship and walls of Jerusalem and rebuilt the city . Still there was no king from the house of David.

What happened to these promises that were promised to David and to Abraham? What happened to these promises that were written in the law about a divine relationship between the house of David and God, himself, in which there would be a continuation forever of the throne of David? What happened is that while they were in exile God promised to continue and fulfill these promises which He gave to their forefathers hundreds of years earlier. Some of these promises were already foretold by Isaiah the prophet in Isaiah 9:6-7.

In these passages we see five titles (four that have survived before us) that describe that child and His relationship to the people and to God. Those titles were the crucial titles that were given to the kings of Egypt. Very similar titles are found in the Egyptian hieroglyphics from the el-Amarna period (1250 - 1350 BCE.).

Let's look at Isaiah 9:6-8:

> *"For a child will be born to us, a son will be given to us; and the government will rest on His shoulders; and His name will be called Wonderful Counselor, Mighty God, Eternal Father, Prince of Peace. There will be no end to the increase of His government or of peace , on the throne of David and over*

his kingdom, to establish it and to uphold
it with justice and righteousness from then
on and forevermore. The zeal of the Lord of
hosts will accomplish this. The Lord sends a
message against Jacob, and it falls on Israel."

What these verses are telling us is that at the
end of a period of great turmoil and war and
conquering armies would comfort the people by
a child that would be born unto them (the
Jewish nation). The government would rest on His
shoulders (He would make the decisions) and His
name would be Wonderful Counselor, Mighty God,
Eternal Father, Prince of Peace. His throne would
be the throne of David and His kingdom would
be set in justice and righteousness and would be
forever.

This kind of king did not exist in Israel, neither
in the days of Isaiah the prophet, Ahaz, Hezekiah
or in any other period of the royal reign in Israel.
In other words, we never had a king like this.
All our kings None of our kings were deserving
of having such titles as a Mighty God, everlasting
Father, or Prince of Peace. Yet the promise was
such from the time of David, "He will be my Son
and I will be His Father". The promise, from about
720 years after David, is still repeated by Isaiah
the prophet. In other words that hope, that desire,
that wishful thinking that we should have such
a ruler, that we should have such a king was not

a once in a historical occurrence. The people of Israel continually awaited the promise of God to be fulfilled.

Isaiah, the prophet, repeats the same hope with these very strong colors in a very vivid way by giving Him the highest royal titles that can be given and understood by the ancient world. There were no higher titles that a man could have. As you know, the kings in Egypt (pharaohs) were considered to be divine and sons of the highest gods. So when Isaiah uses these titles, he is describing the highest office, the highest position, in history. He puts this passage in the historical context of the throne of David and his kingdom.

Then the people of Israel go into exile. In the exile the prophet Jeremiah repeats the same idea but puts it in a different color. In Jeremiah 23:5, we read, "Behold the days are coming, declares the Lord. shall, raise up for David a righteous Branch; and He will reign as king and act wisely and do justice and righteousness in the land." Jeremiah lived about 700 years after David died (the 8th century tomb was already empty and the bones had rotted away when Jeremiah was still expecting a righteous Branch to be raised in the house of David that would reign as king. Isaiah 1 helps us to understand the significance of the righteous Branch as many passages coincide with the idea that the Messiah is a righteous Branch.

While the people of Israel were in exile God

castigated the bad shepherds (Ezekiel 34) that had brought them into the condition that they were in, These shepherds didn't really care about the sheep. In Ezekiel 34:24 it says,

> *"And I, the Lord, will be their God, and*
> *My servant David will be a prince among*
> *them; I, the Lord, have spoken."*

This prince would call them to walk in green pastures and provide for them all their needs. All the shepherd motifs that we see in the Gospels such as in John 7, "my sheep know my voice and I recognize my sheep" are based on the idea of the good shepherd that is described in Ezekiel 34. Jesus is consciously teaching that He is the fulfillment of that good Shepherd from the house of David that will rule his people.

In Ezekiel 36 we read that the people of Israel would go to exile and while there they would be given a new heart and a new spirit. The heart of stone would be removed from their flesh and they would be given a heart of flesh. In other words they would be given a human heart that understands, that is soft, that accepts the love of God that God is willing to give to them. In Ezekiel 37: 24-26 the promise is repeated,

> *"And My servant David will be king over them,*
> *and they will all have one shepherd; walk in*

*My ordinances, and keep my statutes, and
observe them. And they shall live on the land
that I gave to Jacob, My servant, in which your
fathers lived; and they will live on it, they
and their sons, and their sons' sons, forever;
and David My servant shall be their prince
forever. And I will make a covenant of peace
with them; it will be an everlasting covenant
with them. sanctuary in their midst forever."
And I will place them and multiply them, and
will set My sanctuary in the midst forever."*

In other words what He is saying here is that I will
dwell in them forever. This is a prophet teaching in
exile hundreds of years after David. The children
of Israel were not dwelling in the land. They were
suffering and saying how can we sing joy unto the
Lord when we are in exile. They were in misery. Yet
the prophet is telling them that when they return
to the land God is going to give them a shepherd,
His servant David, and He will be one shepherd in
the land. The result of this shepherding would be
that God would dwell inside the people.

In other words, if we are to develop and
understand the idea of Kingship in the New
Testament and the Kingship of Yeshua, we must
understand this concept in the Old Testament. As
you know Yeshua died and on top of His cross was
written "King of the Jews." On what basis did they
call Him "King of the Jews?" He was called "King

of the Jews" on the basis of the prophetic words which God had given hundreds of years earlier about a Davidic king that would rule forever, that would change the heart of the people from a heart of stone to a heart of flesh, that would give them a new Spirit, a Spirit of God. That Davidic king would be their shepherd, their ruler, and would do justice and righteousness in the land.

These were the expectations of the Jewish people. Andrew came to Peter in John 1 and said "we have found that Messiah." Peter immediately left his net and started following this Galilean Jew by the name of Yeshua. This was a revolutionary thing. The fact that we are Messianic Jews today, that we believe in the God of Israel and in Abraham and in King David and that we are reading this Jewish book, we owe to that revolution. If it wasn't for that Galilean Jew who fulfilled those promises, became the divine King which God had promised to the children of Israel by prophecy, died for our sins and atoned for us we would all be idolaters. The new Kingdom which God established in that king was that which He had promised the prophets of Israel.

All of the passages in the New Testament like I Timothy 6:15 are a result of the promises which God had given to Abraham and to David and which were fulfilled in the person of Yeshua Ha-Massiah. He truly brought an eternal Kingdom. This Kingdom fulfilled the desire of God and the desire of man.

The children of Israel had God as their ruler. When they were in the wilderness God ruled and judged them. When they were hungry He fed them. They had enemies. He fought their wars. They needed somebody to judge between a brother and a brother - God gave His law to judge them. God fulfilled all the roles of a King while He was leading them by His hand out of the land of Egypt.

Everything that a king could do God did better. In spite of that they wanted to be like everybody else and us a king like every other nation. So God gave them kings and the kings brought destruction and exile. In the end, through Yeshua Ha-Mashiach God becomes their king again. Just like it was before they asked to be like everybody else - to be like the Gentiles.

In Yeshua Ha-Mashiach we have the unification of the idea of having a King that is both flesh and blood and divine. Therefore that Kingdom is still the same as it was when the children of Israel had a direct relationship between them and God. God has given us a new heart and a new spirit and like He promised in Ezekiel He dwells in us. So God is very much our King today, through Yeshua Ha-Massiah, and we are His citizens, His subjects. Sometimes we, like the children of Israel , like to rebel. Sometimes we shut our eyes and ears and don't want to hear our King. But eventually we all must.

All these ideas of Kingship are something that we are going to have to experience in the second coming. Yeshua came as the Lamb of God in the first coming. His second coming will be as a royal king riding on a horse coming to judge, not to forgive, by righteous standards. It is imperative for us to understand the idea and concept of the Kingship of God in our life and Yeshua as the King of Kings and Lord of Lords.

LIVING STONES

From Teaching from Zion, Vol 1, No. 12, February 1985

Stones are something which Israel has plenty of. In fact, in Jerusalem the building code is "STONE", i.e. all buildings must be made of stone. So, the building at "Netivyah" is also made of stone.

There is a Jewish tradition which states that from the rock on which Abraham sacrificed Issac the world was created. This same rock the Muslims hold to be the rock, in the Mosque of Omar (Dome of the Rock), from which Mohamad sprang to heaven on his horse.

However, Peter teaches us from the Scriptures,

"Behold I lay in Zion a choice stone, a precious corner, and he who believes in Him shall not be disappointed." (Isa. 28:16)
This precious value, then, is for y o u who believe but for those who disbelieve."

The Stone which the builders rejected,

> *has become the very cornerstone", and "a*
> *stone of stumbling and a rock of offense".*
> *(Psalms 118:22 and Isa. 8:14).*

Yeshua is the Rock of whom the prophets have spoken.

He is also called a Rock in I Cor. 10:4,

> *"for they were drinking from a spiritual*
> *rock...and the Rock was the Messiah".*

What is the significance of "Rock" in the Bible? Of course, the first meaning of the Hebrew word **"Zur"** is a rock or stone cliff .The surprising thing is that in the Hebrew Bible out of the 74 times that **"Zur"** or Rock is used, 3 times it is used figuratively for God. This means that almost half of the times that "rock" is used in the Old Testament it refers to God. (See Deut. 32:15; I Sam. 2:2; II Sam 22:32, 47, 23:3; Ps. 18:32, 62:8, 73:26, 78:35....)

If the New Testament writers see fit to call the Messiah "Rock", it must be for the spiritual significance of "The Rock". Yeshua's "rock" characteristics are:

1. He can take abuse.

2. A rock is dependable.

3. A rock is durable.

4. A rock is useful. It can be used for building. It can be used for destruction.

In I Peter chapter 2, we are also called "living rocks". This means that we are "being built up into a spiritual house". Of course, being "living rocks" would mean that some of those "rock" characteristics ought to be ours as well.

It is time for us here in Israel to become more like the "Rock" - to be hard, dependable, useful, durable . . . e t c . We are now facing some difficult times. The Yad L'achim extremists, an Orthodox Jewish organization, has been redeployed with much more sophisticated methods.

They have a giant computer into which they feed every bit of information about any "Christian" or evangelistic effort among Jews. They have paid field people who attend services and make friendships to gather this information and later to harass.

The government agencies are again choosing to close their eyes to the illegal harassment which the Orthodox Jews are giving to "believers". In the last months, "Jewish believers" have been harassed in the following ways:

1. Threatening phone calls

2. Demonstrations in front of people's houses

3. Threatening letters to the employers of believers. If the employers do not fire the "Christians", the employers themselves will

suffer.

4. The intelligence service of the income tax has been sent letters withfalse information about the income of "Christians" in Israel.

5. There has been false complaints of noise and disturbance of peace in homes and places of worship of "Christians"

6. Man handlings....

7. Articles in the newspapers with slander and false accusations. etc.

"Netivyah" has received a letter from the City stating that we must stop meeting for worship in our building because we are violating the zoning laws. **We did not stop!!!** The whole area is in zoning violation. There is not a single building in the whole neighborhood which does not have an office or synagogue . We kept quiet and let our lawyer deal with this. However the Yad L'achim, themselves, called the newspaper and wrote an article called "The New Method of Yad L'achim" to Stop Missionaries". In this article, they admitted that the letter sent to us by the City was a new form of harassment that they are proud to use.

But we, with God's help, like a "rock" will not move. In fact, God is giving us an increase. Last week new people obeyed the Gospel and became believers. We are growing in numbers and also in zeal for God's Kingdom. The Bible Studies are growing and the services are full. We praise the Lord. We ask you to praise the Lord with us.

There is something however, which drags us down. Marcia's illness. As you know she is suffering from rheumatoid arthritis. The doctors have finally come to the conclusion that the time for surgery has arrived. Her hip joint is totally finished. Since she is young, they feel that she should have one of the most modern surgical developments in hip replacement - a cementless prosthesis of the hip joint. However, such surgery has not yet been done in Israel. Only doctors in the U.S.A. and Switzerland have experience with this kind of surgery. The surgeon at Hadassah Hospital in Jerusalem has suggested that they invite an expert on cementless surgery from abroad and let him use Marcia to demonstrate the technique to the Israeli doctors. This would, of course, save us a big expense. I feel that an expert who would be invited would do a better job in a demonstration since he would be surrounded by other surgeons. Please pray with us that this goes well and with God's blessings. They say that it is important for Marcia to have this kind of surgery because when it wears out it can be replaced without so much trouble. The other surgery which uses cement is very difficult to take out and replace.

God make us your living Rocks - - built together into a living building.

WHAT IS HAPPENING TO THE JEWISH PEOPLE?

From Teaching from Zion, Vol 1, No. 12, February 1985

"What is happening to the Jewish people?" is an a la mode question in young intellectual Jewish circles. The large Jewish population of the Diaspora living in London, Paris, or New York talk much about Jewish identity and Jewish roots. We are witnesses to the quiet revolution in Judaism. A revolution in which Israel is the "casus belli", the provoker of conflict. Israel made the Jews in the world neurotics. This is not the neurosis of eschatological expectations like Rabbi Judah HaLevi had when he said: "I am in the west and my heart is in the east". In the days of Rabbi Judah Halevi, the Jews did not have an existing state in the land of their forefathers. He couldn't have come even if he wanted to. Even if Rabbi Halevi could have found a way to arrive in Jaffa port, he wouldn't have found many Jews there.

Today, thank God, there is a Jewish State with over three million Jews. Nothing stops a Jew, from the free world, of packing up his pack, boarding a plane or ship and arriving in the "promised land". This very possibility, this very need to make a choice causes neurosis both for the Jews who live in and the Jews who are still in the Diaspora.

Those who are in Israel are frustrated by their living here and the existence of a rich successful Diaspora which does not have 1500% inflation and no 35 days a year army reserve. Even the Orthodox Jews who ought to have been the first to get on the bandwagon of immigration to Israel didn't. In fact, the opposite is true. The majority of the big rabbis and Hasidic courts are still ambiguous about the State of Israel and their relationship to it.

The Messianic Jews are no exception to this neurosis. We have a lot of talk about Jewish identity and much ado about Israel and returning to the roots. But, in reality, they like the Lubavitcher rabbi and the Satmar Hassid are very comfortable in the Diaspora. David Clayman, the head of the American Jewish Congress Israel office in Jerusalem, said: "Israel has become the religion of American Jewry, but it is not their sole interest". If it were, they would come to live here.

This is a particularly dangerous thing which is happening to the Jewish people. "Israel" as a state and a political system is almost replacing the Almighty God. One of the people with whom i have very little sympathy, Rabbi Joelish Teitelbaum of Satmer, said in his book Va Yoel Moshe "the very idea of Israel's receiving a government by themselves, before the coming of the Messiah, involves heresy and denial of the ways of the Holy One, blessed be He, since only He - God - can enslave and redeem; we can have no other redeemer but God in the days of the Messiah". This rabbi from Satmer is not neurotic. He is living in New York City and is totally consistent in his view of the Diaspora and Israel. In violent anger and hatred, he proclaims that Zionism outweighs all the sins of Israel and the world and source of them.

The other side, that is also totally consistent, is that of the Israeli who knows nothing of God nor does he want to know. Israel for him is just another country like all the countries of the world. For such, Israel is just an accident into which he was accidentally born and which when he finishes the Army he will have to go and see what the world has to offer. You might find such Israelis farming on the banks of the Amazon river or as mercenaries in Africa. Two things will be common in them: no faith in God and no special feeling for Israel.

The rabbi of Satmer (an ultra-Orthodox Jew) and the totally secular Israeli are both healed from the neurosis which afflicts most of us Jews. Howard

Cossel, former president of the American Jewish Community, said in a recent television interview: "The Jewish people are most obsessed with their Jewishness".

The question **"Who Is a Jew?"** is a question which arises from the complexity of problems that the very existence of a Jewish state poses. Today in America there is a bias - "if you do not learn Hebrew and don't come to Israel you are not really Jewish". This bias is exploited by the fundraising experts of the United Jewish Agency in order to get those Jews who feel guilty about not coming to Israel to give more dollars. In a way, it is the milking of our neurotic attitudes. In a way, it pacifies the conscience of those Jews - allowing them to live still in the United States and to feel Jewish and good about giving.

All this is an introduction! Hillel Zeitlin, of blessed memory, in his poem inspired by the expectancy of the Messiah, wrote: "star calls to star - behold the harbinger of salvation! Thunder cries out to thunder - the Son of Man from the heavens! Mountain to Mountain - its heartbeats are heard; way to way - his footsteps are revealed"! This Jewish neurosis is a result of not seeing nor understanding what Hillel Zeitlin expressed so aptly in his poem. How long will many, even pious Jews, persist in their refusal to accept the Messianic message revealed to us? This message which in the 2000 years of Diaspora has ground us to dust and made us as dung in the streets; and the miracle of our uprising has given us a place among the nations and enabled us to begin the liberation and ingathering of the remnants of Israel unto Zion.

We believe that in Israel God is acting to fulfill his Messianic promises. This is already taking place. Through our cooperation with the All Mighty, blessed be He, the solution to our existence as Jews will be a reality without this split allegiance.

In other words, as Messianic Jews we ought to overcome the neurosis of "who is a Jew" of "my body is in the United States but my heart in Jerusalem". We ought to see that God is at work in the history of Israel and wants us to be partners with Him in the inauguration of the Messianic age for Israel.

We cannot be consistent in our own minds with respect to being Jewish believers in Yeshua, having a new heart, and having the peace of the Messiah in us unless we see that everything, which is our task, is given to us by God for the bringing of the Messiah to Israel. If we are blind and do not see the hand and the calling of God in our lives - we are the most neurotic of all Jews. Let us aim and hit the mark.

HOPE IS NEVER ILL
WHEN FAITH IS WELL

From Teaching from Zion, Vol.1, No 13, June 1985.

This is a statement from John Bunyan which has proven to be most true in our experience. Marcia is home and walking now with only one crutch. We are so grateful to God and to our brothers and sisters who were so generous to us during Marcia's hospitalization in the U.S.A. We did not expect to receive any help from the brethren in order to pay the medical bills. It was a real grace from God that so many people have given us such great help. Marcia's father was going to pay for the hospitalization by himself with a loan from the bank. We are especially thankful that we could return some of this loan early. The donations that the brothers gave covered 65% of the operation cost and that was far more than we expected. We are thankful to God for all this love that you have shared with us by helping us meet our bills. We are also thankful to the elders of Newland Street congregation and to Ruby Little who wrote the letter to the elders on her sole initiative. Had we known that she was doing something like that we would have stopped it because of our pride. As it was, it was too late to do so and the elders had approved of it. We are resigned to the fact that God works in mysterious ways to perform his wonders. The really great thing is that Marcia is able to walk again and live without pain. We took our first outdoor trip with the young people from our congregation on Pentecost and Marcia was able to walk and fellowship throughout the whole day. It was wonderful to have her participation with the rest of the congregation and not to have to leave her alone at home. Praise be to God!

I would like to share with you one of the more exciting things that is happening in Jerusalem. "Netivyah" is starting a major project of writing a Hebrew Jewish commentary of the New Testament. You might ask, why is this so exciting? Well, there is no existing Hebrew commentary on the New Testament. There is no Jewish commentary in either Hebrew or English which has been written in over 100 years. The British and Foreign Bible Society has received market research on the "Attitudes to Scriptures in Israel". The results are surprising:

Ownership of Religious Books
Old Testament   95%
Jewish Prayer Book 81%
Talmud 41%

New Testament 12%
Koran 3%

A recent UNESCO report (JP June 14, 1984) finds that Israelis are the most frequent book readers among all the peoples of the world. More books are being published in Israel per capita than in any other country. In this market study, The people were asked about reading the Bible. 20% answered that they read the Bible "Very often" and 28% said 'sometimes'. In a similar study that was done in West Germany in 1978, only 15% of the people read the Bible 'very often'. The study also shows that half of the Bibles which Israelis possess are bound together with the New Testament. Two questions in the survey referred to the people's tolerance of the New Testament in Israel.

On the question of use of the New Testament in schools, 9% answered 'very desirable', 34% 'desirable', 22% 'not so desirable' and 34% 'not desirable at all'. Of the Israelis who read the New Testament, only 11% felt that they understood the material.

ONE OF THE GREATEST NEEDS IS A HEBREW JEWISH COMMENTARY OF THE NEW TESTAMENT.

Most Israelis look at the New Testament as some negative, "Christian", foreign, non-Jewish book. We need to put the New Testament back into the first century Jewish world in which it was written. Jews need to be able to see that Jesus is not made in California or in Rome.

When I shared this need with Dr. David Flusser, from the Hebrew University, and with other scholars, they all just about jumped from joy. The response of those with whom we talked was that "Israel needs such a commentary as do most Christians because they also need to know the BOOK from the first century perspective".

We want a Hebrew commentary to be present in every home in Israel. In order to do this, we must have some important ingredients:

A.   It must be scholastic on a commercial level.
B. Jews and Christians must work on it together so that it can be objective and not considered as strictly "Missionary Propaganda".
C.   It must deal with the text of the New Testament only in light of the first century and not be a platform for missionary propaganda.
D. It should be published in Israel by a regular reputable commercial publishing company.

Some of these ingredients might be hard to understand. This might especially be true with "b" which states that Jews and Christians need to work together. However, you must understand that:

a.   If only Christians would be writing it, it would be automatically suspect for unobjective treatment of the subject.

b.   We need the rabbinical Jewish input in order to relate better to the world of Jesus.

c.   We need high level scholastic input which will make this kind of commentary commercially desirable.

Highly respected Jewish scholars with whom we have talked have agreed to work with us because they feel that it is important for Israelis to know that Jesus is a part of our most valuable Jewish heritage.

The commentary will have a number of important elements which will make it unique. It will have the parallels from the Jewish literature relating to the New Testament. Both linguistic, historical and cultural notations will be provided for the reader right on the page of the commentary. This Jewish material will be a great help in explaining things which the Western reader cannot see without the knowledge of Hebrew and Greek. The commentary will also have on each page archaeological and geographic notes which will help him when he is traveling in the location of the events. One will be able to actually take the commentary and use it as a guide book.

We already have an orthodox Jewish rabbi who has agreed to work with us full   time on this project.

He is a researcher in the Hebrew University and a student of the New Testament for 16 years. He started to study the New Testament when he took a correspondence course that I wrote and published in Hebrew in 1969. We are concluding a contract with this rabbi next week. He will start to work right-a-way on the commentary. We have to pay $900 per month to this rabbi and we will also have other expenses soon. At this point, all that we are doing is being done by faith. We have weighed the situation very carefully and we do not want congregations to give mission funds for this project. We would like foundations and individuals to give towards this project. The accountant says that we need $120,000 for the period of six years so that we can give about $25,000 a year in salaries and keep the project going. Soon, Lord willing, we will have a brochure out, with some examples, which will explain the project and give a better idea of the commentary.

If Israel is going to change its relationship to Jesus, it will have to see Jesus as a Jew in the context of the first century Jewish world. Such a commentary will be a great help in unwrapping the Western Christian wrapping in which Jesus has been wrapped and kept distant from Israel.

Please keep us in your prayers and keep Jerusalem in your hearts.

WAS JESUS A PHARISEE?

From Teaching from Zion, Vol.1, No 13, June 1985.

The question of the Pharisees in the first century has been treated unfairly by many "Christian" scholars because of the strong exhortation and critique of the Pharisees in the New Testament. Now, in the last years, attention has again been focused on the Jewishness of Jesus and his relationship with the people of Israel. Many books have been published on the subject. Here is a short list of some of the famous titles:

Jesus the Jew by Gerza Vermes.
Jesus and the Pharisee by John Bowker.
Rabbinic Traditions About the Pharisees Before 70 by Jacob Neusner.
Christian Origins and Judaism by W.D. Davies.
The Jewish Background of Christianity by David Daube.

Of course, these are just a few titles from many books written by both Jews and Gentiles. Their significance is not only what is written in them but also that "Christian" scholars are involved with the Jewishness of the New Testament and Jewish scholars with Jesus as a Jew.

Right at the outset of this short article, I will give you my thesis:

1. Jesus was in many respects a Pharisee. He believed in angels. He believed in the resurrection. He believed that God's revelation is progressive and dynamic.

2. Pharisees from the extreme right wing "Beit Shammai" were out to get Jesus.

3. Jesus was seen by the two leading factions of the Pharisees as an upstart making his own brand of Pharisaism. This is the reason for their strong opposition.

TO CALL UPON THE NAME OF THE LORD

From Teaching from Zion, Vol 1, Issue 14, October 1985

In the previous issue of the "Teaching From Zion" we informed you about the Hebrew Jewish commentary of the New Testament and told you about Rabbi Menachem Rubin who is working with "Netivyah" on this project. We have mailed a brochure about the project and have requested people to participate financially in the support of this project. In the first few weeks after the brochure was mailed out, we have been blessed with $700 for this project. Naturally, the amount of $700 does not cover the cost of Rabbi Rubin's salary but we do hope that as time passes and the work progresses that more people will want to have a part in this commentary.

You see, one of the important things about this work is the Jewish perspective of the New Testament text which is surfacing. Let me give you a small example of such Jewish understanding. *"To*

Call Upon the Name of the Lord" is a technical term of the First Century Jewish world for the recitation of the "Shema" (Deut. 6:4). If this is true we must look at passages like Romans 10:12-13.

> *"For there is no distinction between Jew and Greek; for the same Lord is Lord of all abounding in riches for all who call upon Him; for "WHOEVER WILL CALL UPON THE NAME OF THE LORD WILL BE SAVED".*

As you will note, verse 13 is actually a quotation from Joel 2:32. Joel "Lord" is actually "Jehovah". This makes the point which Paul is making much clearer and also different from the standard Baptist doctrine which says that just saying a prayer in Jesus name will save you.

Paul's point in verse 12 is God's equality to all. Everyone who calls upon Him will be delivered. In other words, abandoning idolatry and doing the "SHEMA" will deliver you from God's judgment. The word for "saved" in Hebrew is "Imalet" which means "will escape". The same root is used later in the same verse to describe the "Remnant". "Remnant" here has the same meaning as "saved" in modern Protestant vocabulary.

Let's look at another passage which has the same phrase "to call upon the name of the Lord" in II Timothy 2:19.

"But, God's firm foundation stands bearing this seal, 'The Lord knows those who are His', and 'let everyone who names the name of the Lord depart from iniquity.'"

This verse has a quotation from <u>Numbers 16:5</u> and <u>Ben Sira 17:26</u>. (Ben Sira is a Jewish, non-Biblical book held in high respect by both Jews and Christians). <u>Ben Sira</u> 17:26 is based on a quotation from Isaiah 26:13 and comes from a context of repentance from the works of idolatry. The writer affirms that if a person turns by word of mouth to God and departs from iniquity he will be delivered, i.e. "saved".

The Hebrew word for "delivered" means also "saved". In II Timothy 2:19 Paul talks about a "seal" in "God's firm foundation" This "seal" has two parts. One part is that "The Lord knows those who are His". The second part is that "Let everyone who names the name of the Lord depart from iniquity". The meaning of which is let those who (say the Shema) affirm the one God and commit to keep his commandments also depart from iniquity.

I cannot bring to you all the ancient Jewish sources supporting this but I feel that understanding such a small thing like the First Century meaning of "calling upon the name of the Lord" can help us deepen our faith. It must be mentioned that this understanding of the passage helps us to greatly see the divinity of the Messiah in passages like <u>I</u> <u>Cor.1:2</u>,

> *"...called to be saints together with all those who in every place call on the name of our Lord Yeshua HaMassiach both their Lord and ours".*

From time to time in the "Teaching From Zion" we are going to bring before you such discoveries which we have made together with Rabbi Rubin. However, if we are to realize this project to the end it will depend on the support which we receive from you and your friends in the Messiah.

During the last weeks of August and the first week of September I was not in Jerusalem. Two weeks in Finland and one week in Spain was a period full of excitement. In Finland Ahuvah Ben Meier and I held two seminars - one in Karmel Koti and the second in Kouvola. In addition to the seminars we traveled a fair distance speaking every night in a different city.

The unusual thing about this trip to Finland was that seven people from America came all the way to Finland to see what the Lord is doing. Dr. J. P. Sanders, David East, Dr. Timothy Tucker and his wife, Maria, Ernest O. Stewart, and Wallace Mays and his wife, Virginia were no regular tourists. For five days they tracked Rev. Paavoli Toivio, Ahuvah and myself over the back roads of Finland.   They stayed in the homes of Finnish brothers and sisters and some even ate fresh smoked salmon on the edge of the lake. Most of their time was spent in most serious discussions with the brothers and sisters. For many of those American brothers this was a new experience in a new country. The newness of their experience can be summarized in one phrase - "they saw a restoration movement in the making".

Brother Juan Monroy invited me to come to Spain in order to speak in the Spanish Lectureship for leaders of the local congregations. I knew from the beginning that it would be an exciting time for me in Spain. I had no idea it would turn out to be so exciting. The first day that I arrived in Madrid, in the first hour, I was flimflammed off of $1,000 by a sting operation that a 64-year-old woman and two younger men did on me.

The second day brother Monroy took me to Escorial, the place that the Spanish kings had their palaces, for the conference. To be with 170 leaders of the Spanish Restoration Movement and to talk about Jesus King of the Jews in Spanish was just about enough to make my pump overload. You see, in 1492 my forefathers were thrown out of Spain because they didn't want to convert to Christianity. Now almost five hundred years later a Jew from Jerusalem comes to Spain in the name of Yeshua our Messiah to teach Spanish people who have left the Roman church about Jesus and Israel. I spoke in Spanish or should I say Sephardi Spanish which was the oldest Spanish dialect spoken by the Jews of Castile in the fifteenth century.

It was a historical occasion for me - as if the circle had been completed. Five hundred years ago the Catholic church persecuted my forefathers for not accepting their false "Christianity". Now a Jew goes back to Spain to teach them about the true Jesus, Messiah and king of Israel - not of Rome.

The Spanish brothers were more than gracious to me. They took up the largest collection ever taken in these conferences and gave me back the money that was robbed from me in Madrid.

If you think that this was enough excitement you are wrong. One morning brother Anderson and brother Sinclair and their wives went with me as a tourist to see the palaces of Escorial. In the library of King Philip II of Spain we saw a beautiful Hebrew manuscript. Being a typical Israeli, it was not enough to see it through the glass, so I asked if I could hold it in my hand. The attendant at the Royal Library said, "come tomorrow morning at 10:00 a.m.". She probably thought that she would never see me again. But at 10:15 a.m. the next day I was there. She called the monsignor and he took me to room and locked me in and asked me what I wanted. "The Hebrew manuscript," I said. He said, "which ones?" Just bring some was my answer.

After a few minutes an attendant came with about six big heavy leather-bound tomes. My heart was running fast - here were books written by the hand of Jews who lived in Spain over five hundred years ago. The first volume was opened and my eyes ran down the beautiful Hebrew handwriting. "Yeshua Mashiach"- Jesus the Christ in Hebrew were the first words on which my eyes stopped. The name of the book cannot be divulged now but it was written sometime between the 12th and 14th century in Hebrew with the vowel signs. It contains material from the Jewish literature which proves that Yeshua is the Messiah. It has no passages from the New Testament at all and Yeshua Mashiach is mentioned only twice in the book. The book also does not have the standard prophetic passages which "Christians" have used as proof text.

The material is brought by a Jew who knew the targum in Aramaic, the Talmud, and the Midrashim by heart. The writer must have been a rabbi who became a believer in Yeshua Mashiach. The book was originally written in order to teach the "Christians" how to witness Jesus to Jews, to show that the teachings of Jesus and the teachings about Jesus were not strange to Jews and Judaism.

After looking and reading the book for over two hours I asked the priest if I could photocopy it. He said, "No"! But if you want it on microfilm we could arrange it for you."

The photographer of the palace came and we talked about the price - agreed - and I wrote the check. I also asked the priest for publication rights. Would you believe it? We got the publication rights and, Lord willing, we will publish it soon.

Such a book is invaluable. The research which I made has shown that the book was unknown - until now! The material in the book is original and in our day and age it shows the deepest form of Judaism to be in no contradiction with the New Testament. This book has been the height of my excitement these last few weeks.

On November 4, 1985, "Netivyah" stood trial before the magistrate court of Jerusalem. We have been taken by the City as a test case for zoning violation. However, all involved in the case know beyond the shadow of a doubt that the "Yad L'achim ", a radical orthodox organization, stands behind this case. We need your prayers for justice to be made in Jerusalem and for our freedom as Jews who believe in the Messiah to be preserved. We, at this time, want to keep everything in as low key as possible. We want you to be mentally prepared for a long and difficult fight. In fact, we might have to call upon you soon to write to the State Department, your congressmen, and the Israeli Ambassador on our behalf. Right now and first of all, we want you to take this matter in prayer to our Heavenly Father. We are counting on your support and love to continue this fight.

With much love to all of you,

P.S. While I was absent from Jerusalem, one of the most important things was that brother Powlison, brother Spiro, and others from the Jerusalem congregation carried on the work beautifully.

A CASE OF MISTAKEN I.D.

From Teaching from Zion, Vol 1, Issue 14, October 1985

"Identity -

1) the set of behavioral or personal characteristics by which an individual is recognizable;

2) the quality or condition of being exactly the same as something else".

This is the way that **Roget's Thesaurus** defines "identity". I feel that this definition, as partial as it may be, will be of help for the understanding of the problem - "A Case of Mistaken I.D."

Last month a man speaking good Hebrew called me and asked if he could come and talk to me about a particular problem. When he came to Jerusalem and presented his problem, darkness overtook me. The problem was "how can I change my identity card from Jewish to 'Christian'?". Naturally, the first question was "Why"? His answer was, "I believe in Yeshua and now I am no longer a Jew". I became temperamentally disagreeable. My years of study and involvement had taught me the background of such attitudes as this Israeli Jew expressed.

You see, the real problem was not this brother's mistaken idea about his identity in the Messiah. The real problem is the wrong theology which some Christians hold in relationship to the New Testament and to the Jewish people. In order to understand the issue, I want to go into a little history and theology of the New Testament.

The history of the problem is thus. The Catholic Church had a long-standing history of antisemitism. This bad attitude about the Jews came about from two main sources. The first was the pre-Christian hate that Gentiles had against the Jews. We see this hate in Haman's attitude toward the Jews as it is written in the book of Esther 3:8 "There is a certain people scattered and dispersed among the peoples in all the provinces of your kingdom; and their laws are different from those of all other people, and they do not observe the king's laws, so it is not in the king's interest to let them remain." This pre-Christian hate which permeated the Greco-Roman world did not get expunged with the advent of political Christianity in the days of Constantine when the Roman

Empire converted to "Christianity".

The second expression of this hate against the Jews was the theology of "New Israel = The Church". A teaching that holds that Israel no longer really exists and that the church has taken the place of Israel. Naturally, such a teaching is contradictory to the direct Word of God.

> *"I say then, God has not rejected His people, has He? May it never be! For I too am an Israelite, a descendant of Abraham, of the tribe of Benjamin— From the standpoint of the Gospel they are enemies for your sake, but from the standpoint of God's choice they are beloved for the sake of the fathers." (Romans 11:1, 28).*

This teaching, although it started in the Catholic church, was much more influential in protestant theology. It has even been taken up without reexamination by those who claim to be intent on restoring the First Century Church. In the protestant world the idea that Israel and all that is connected with it is finished was strongly advocated by dispensational theology. However, as I said earlier, this was just an inheritance left behind by the Catholic heritage. The bad thing about this theology was not in the ideological level but in the practical application that it took toward the Jews.

In the Catholic church it brought about the

Inquisition, the forced conversion of the Jews at the pain of death, and the teaching that Judaism was a demonic religion that must be totally abandoned upon admission of Jesus as the Christ.

Jews who really wanted to accept Yeshua as the Messiah had to sign such statements as the following:

"I do here and now renounce every rite and observance of the Jewish religion, detesting all its most solemn ceremonies and tenets that in former days I kept and held. In (the) future I will practice no rite or celebration connected with it, nor any custom of my past error, promising neither to seek it out nor to perform it. Further do I renounce all things forbidden or detested by Christian teaching. And, In the name of this Creed, which I truly believe and hold with all my heart, I promise that I will never return to the vomit of Jewish superstition. Never again will I fulfill any of the offices of Jewish ceremonies to which I was addicted, nor ever more hold them dear. I altogether deny and reject the errors of the Jewish religion, casting forth whatever conflicts with the Christian Faith, and affirming that my belief in the Holy Trinity is strong enough to make me live the truly Christian life, shun all intercourse with other Jews and have the circle of my friends always eat Christian food, and as a genuinely devout Christian go often and reverently to Church. I promise also to maintain and embrace with due love and reverence the* observance of all the Lord's days or feasts for martyrs as declared by the piety of the Church, and upon those days to consort always with sincere Christians, as it behooves a pious and sincere Christian to do..." (II Of Erwig, from Leg. Vis. 12.3.14)

This is what Jews would have to sign when they would become "Christians".

THIS IS THE ROOT OF THE MODERN ATTITUDE THAT SAYS THAT JEWS WHO BELIEVE IN YESHUA AS THEIR MESSIAH HAVE LOST THEIR IDENTITY AS JEWS.

It is true that when a Jew accepts Yeshua as the Messiah he becomes a Christian but it is not true that he stops being a Jew. This is true for these reasons:

a.   A Christian in the New Testament means a disciple of the Messiah. We all would agree that there are Chinese Christians, black Christians, and Korean Christians. We all would agree that each <u>nationality</u> has the right to keep their national holy-days and eat their national foods. This naturally would fall under the teaching of Saint Paul, "I have become all things to all men, that I may by all means save some." (read I Cor. 9:19-23)

But when it comes to the Jews somehow this principle well understood in other contexts gets lost. The pagan nations still keep pagan holidays like "Christmas" and "Easter" and have fertility symbols like painted eggs in their homes but Jews who believe in the Messiah must give up their national identity, food, and relationship in order to be saved.

b. Reflection upon the book of Acts is proof that the early Jewish The Christians - or - Messianic Jews did not cut their relationship with the Jewish community nor did they stop going to the synagogue, nor did they stop keeping the Jewish feasts of History. James meets Paul in Acts 21:20, 24:14-18 and in a way boasts before Paul that there are so many "The Christians" in Jerusalem and they are all zealous for the Law. Paul, then to prove that the accusation that came against him was false, goes to the Temple in Jerusalem and offers "offerings", takes a vow, and even pays the money for four others to do the same with him. In Acts 20:16 we find Paul in a hurry to get to Jerusalem for the Feast of Pentecost, which is the feast of the first fruit. He brings the "first fruit" of the Gentile The Christians to Jerusalem as a sign of the oneness in the Messiah.

c.   Some people might say "how could you do things and keep feasts which are a part of the Old Law and still be under the grace of the Messiah?" Well, the grace of the Messiah has to do with our salvation and it is the only means by which we may be "saved". It does not change a person's cultural background. We all know that the New Covenant is now in effect and that no person can be saved by works of the Law. Naturally we would oppose any person keeping any "commandments" with the idea that the "keeping of commandments" can or will bring him any benefit in respect to salvation. All our works are as filthy rags. All this put together still does not deny the right and the privilege of Jews who do believe in Yeshua as the Messiah and who do suffer for righteousness sake in His name to have the same identity that Paul, Timothy and John had in the Messiah - Jewish identity.

d.   You ought to know that the attitude held by many brothers which deny Jews to be Jewish in their lifestyle is based on false teaching not written in the New Testament and which is contradictory to both the Spirit of God's Word and the Letter of God's Word. This attitude is based on the Catholic tradition of hatred for Jews and Judaism. It feeds on passages of scripture taken out of their context. It wants to build back the middle wall of the partition in the opposite direction from the First Century.

In the first century Jewish believers wanted to Judaize the Gentiles and Paul wrote Galatians, Ephesians and Colossians to fight this trend. In the 20th century, the Gentiles want to Gentilize the Jews. They believe that keeping of the

Messiahmas (Xmas) is not a religious holiday although it is a pagan vessel filled with a little of "The Christian" filling. However, when a Jewish brother wants to keep the memory of the time that God freed his nation from slavery and brought them into the Promised Land, those Gentile Christians who do not understand God's word want to deny them this right. Every Jewish believer in the Messiah that I know who keeps the Passover does so with a great desire to witness the Lamb of God who takes away our sins and of the Messiah our real Passover.

My personal experience in the Messiah has been that the Jewish Orthodox would much rather the Jewish believers become Gentilized and not keep any connection with the Jewish community. The Orthodox Jews want to prove that once a Jew accepts Yeshua as the Messiah he no longer is a Jew. Some of the well-meaning but misinformed The Christians fall right into their hands. The Orthodox know that no Gentile The Christian mission will have much of an impact on the Jewish community as a whole.

The Jew does not even have to deal with the issue of Yeshua because the Yeshua of the "Church" is a total stranger to him. However, when a fellow Jew, mind you a real Jew, believes in Yeshua Ha-Yehudim (Yeshua King of the Jews) you are now talking about family relationship, roots, and the highest dreams a Jew has about salvation. How can a Jew ignore such a problem presented to him by a fellow Jewish brother. This is why the Jewish The Christians in Israel are getting ten times more persecution than the "The Christian Missionaries."

I know that some of these ideas are new to many people who are hearing them for the first time. For this reason I want to return to some of the axiomatic statements of the New Testament The Christianity and show that freedom in the Messiah has nothing to do with whether a person eats Kosher or not or keeps the Passover or not. It does have to do with the right of each The Christian to have his own identity - and not have to eat with a spoon and fork at McDonald's in order to qualify as a "Faithful Sound Brother in the Messiah".

What are the Biblical truths that are essential for our communion as brothers in the Messiah?
   a. Faith in One God, Father of all Creation.
   b. Faith in Yeshua that He is our Messiah.
   c. Submission to the teaching and the personal requirements of the Messiah.
      This point would include in it such things as baptism, the Lord's Supper, and church attendance. However, the outward manner and season of these things could vary from place to place. One place could feel that baptism in a   bathtub is not   right for them. Another place could feel that they would like to meet five times a week and take

communion on Sunday at noon with a great feast of food right after the communion. Some might even feel that communion should not be taken at all in the day time and that it has to be taken at night. Now, all these would be well if people did not try to judge or impose their particular practices on their neighboring community.

We must understand that the Messiah might require something from one group of people, The Christians which he does not require of another group of The Christians. Like for example - the requirements for Men are different from those of Women. The requirements of Older Men are different from those of the Younger Men. The requirements of Elders are different from Deacons. The requirements of the Rich might be different from the Poor. On this same level there might be different requirements for different national groups. This does not mean that they have a different Gospel but that they might have a different job in the body of the Messiah. (One must see Romans 14 in the context of the Jewish-Gentile conflict inside the church of Rome.)

The Way of Salvation is the same for each person and each nation - including Israel. However, the expression of this salvation by the grace of Yeshua our Messiah in cultural setting might be different and should be different in order to reach the whole world. Jews do not have to become

Gentiles in their lifestyle in order to please God. Gentiles do not have to become Jews. We are One in the Messiah. We have one God, one baptism, one spirit, one church, and one Bible.

Look at I Cor. 7:17-24.

> *"Only, as the Lord has assigned to each one, as God has called each, in this manner let him walk. And thus I direct in all the churches. Was any man called already circumcised? Let him not become uncircumcised. Has anyone been called in uncircumcision? Let him not be circumcised. Circumcision is nothing and uncircumcision is nothing. But (what matters is) the keeping of the commandments of God. Let each man remain in that condition in which he was called. Were you called while a slave? Do not worry about it; but if you are able also to become free, rather do that. For who he was called while free is the Messiah's slave. You were bought with a price; do not become slaves of men. Brethren, let each man remain with God in that condition in which he was called."*

You should know that the terms 'circumcision and uncircumcision' stand in the New Testament for Jew and Gentile. So what Paul is demanding here from all the churches is that Jews do not give up their Jewish heritage when they accept the Messiah and that Gentiles do not accept Judaism when they accept the Messiah. Let each remain culturally and ethnically in the state in which God called him.

The Jewish person who wanted to accept the Messiah in order to stop being Jewish was wrong. He was wrong in that he thought that by faith in the Messiah that he could run away from his Jewishness. If all Jews would accept the Messiah would there no longer be Israel? What would the Jews become if they could not be Jews? Should they all become Italians because now they believe in Yeshua? Is there such a thing as a "Christian nationality" that they could belong to after conversion? Could each converted Jew receive a U.S.A, passport?

I do not understand those who teach that a Jew stops being Jewish because he believes that Yeshua is the Messiah, King of the Jews.

It might be that they think that Judaism is only a religion and not a nation. Who gave them the right to decide what is a nation and what is not? We as Jews did not give anyone the right to decide our identity and since we also know God, we have it on the highest authority that He also did not give this job to anybody else.

HUMAN TRADITION AND THE COMMANDMENTS OF GOD

From Teaching from Zion, Vol.1 No 15, February 1986

The relationship of Yeshua to the Pharisees has been in the forefront of Jewish and non-Jewish scholars concerned with the New Testament in context of the first century. It has become the vogue to write about "Jesus and the Pharisees". It is true that Yeshua and the Pharisees had something going between them. Yeshua expected the Pharisees to "know better" and the Pharisees expected Yeshua to buckle under the traditions which were being developed by the sect. It ought to be rioted that Yeshua was closer to the Pharisees both in His theology and in His lifestyle. Precisely, this could be the reason for the numerous confrontations which are recorded in the New Testament between Yeshua and the Pharisees. We are going to examine one of these confrontations and attempt to look at it through the perspective of first century Jewish eyes.

> *"Then some Pharisees and scribes came to Yeshua from Jerusalem, saying, 'Why do your disciples transgress the tradition of the elders? For they do not wash their hands when they eat bread."* [1]

Normally, people only complain and fuss with people whom they have some relationship with. Christians normally criticize other Christian groups. When have you heard a criticism of Buddhism from your pulpit? You do hear, however, criticism of brothers who are not walking exactly in the same path or you may hear criticism of neighboring denominations. In this case, the Pharisees came to Yeshua with criticism about the disciples' behavior. They felt that the disciples should have known better and since they did not that their rabbi, Yeshua, should teach them better.

It is important to note that the Pharisees would not have come with such a criticism unless they thought that:

a) Yeshua would agree with their views about 'hand washing' and

b) that He would teach the disciples to wash their hands before eating. It is interesting to note that 'hand washing' did not become a codified law in Judaism until the early third century.

In other words, this group of Pharisees that came to Yeshua with the complaint were not from the main stream of Pharisaic Jews. Most scholars think that they were from the school of Shamai, "the strictest sect of the Pharisees", in the words of Paul. They had made hand washing a law of their own small sect and it had become their trademark. Hany religious groups develop such traditions which later become a test of fellowship and they become known by these peculiarities.

Back to Jewish law! There was no such law of 'hand washing' in the Law of Moses and not even in the formal Jewish tradition of The Oral Law in Yeshua's time. Of course, the Pharisees knew that. They even called 'hand washing' a 'Tradition of the Elders'. It should be known by now that in most religious circles "Tradition" is observed much more strictly than the direct teaching of the scriptures. This is true in both "Christian" and Jewish circles of religion. People develop traditions which at the end master their relationship with God. This was the case with this small group of Pharisees who came complaining to Yeshua.

Let us now look at the answer which Yeshua gave them.

"Why do you transgress the commandments

of God for the sake of your traditions?"

Which commandment of God did they transgress when they criticized Yeshua's disciples for eating with unwashed hands? I do not think that Yeshua gave, in His answer, a blanket condemnation of the Pharisees. I think so for the following reasons:

a) the fact that the Pharisees were sinners did not give the disciples the right to sin and

b) you cannot make a gross generalization about any public sector that is also true about the Pharisees.

They were no greater sinners than any other religious community. You might be aware that some of these texts which we are discussing have been used as fuel for Anti-Semitic feelings in the "Christian" communities because they have been understood outside the first century Jewish context of events.

The answer that Yeshua gave to the Pharisees was very specific and fitting for this specific case of vain criticism which this particular group of Pharisees were engaging in at that moment. Matthew brings additional support for the trend of breaking God's commandments for the sake of human traditions. Yeshua takes the most difficult case possible, a case which juxtaposes dedication and religious generosity with keeping the commandments. Religious communities are often willing to forego some indiscretions from members who have shown great zeal and dedication.

This is what we have here - a person who gave all his property to the temple. In the time of the second temple in Jerusalem, people could make a "holy trust", i.e. give all their goods to the Temple. They were allowed to continue to use the property and even to benefit from the interest, fruit. The property, however, really belonged to the Temple Trust. This person had given all to the Temple (Korban=Sacrifice) and now he was using this as an excuse for not honoring his aged parents as the commandment requires - "Honor your father and mother..." Of course, the implication here is that this particular sect of Pharisees approved this kind of behavior and by this gave more value to their sectarian teachings than to the explicit word of God. As I stated above, Yeshua brings this as an example of His statement "You yourselves transgress the commandments of God for the sake of your tradition."

Yeshua next brings quotations from the prophet Isaiah in order to substantiate His case. The quotation from Isaiah states two things: a) dedication by speech and lip service does not imply a real heart dedication to God. Nor does giving all as a korban to the Temple imply true relationship with God and b) holding to the doctrines and precepts of men is not worth a thing as far as worshiping God is concerned. Dedication is of value only when God's commands are kept according to His will and not according to human tradition. At this point Yeshua rests His case from the legal point of view. He had given a case in point which proved that they (the Pharisees) respected the "rules of their establishment" more than the Word of God. This was not a new trend. The prophet Isaiah had already warned the people of Israel on the same issue.

Yeshua now turned to the people and gave them a teaching which today is greatly misappropriated. "Not what enters into the mouth defiles the man, but what proceeds out of the mouth, this defiles the man." Most people think that this statement gives a blanket license to eat what you want - "not what enters into the mouth defiles the man". We see that the problem of understanding this statement is solved in Mark by a parenthetical statement "thus He declared all foods clean" (Mark 7:19). The emphasis is on "foods" - not that everything was declared clean and could be put into the mouth. The term food in Greek **"bromatha"** means "eatable" like in Luke 24:41. Of course, different things are considered "edible" by different people. In Hong Kong I saw people eating snakes but for most Americans that would not be considered "edible".

However, back to the context of the statement. This statement is based on the story of Moses and Miriam, his sister, in Numbers 12. Miriam spoke against Moses, her brother, and became a leper. Leprosy is one of the greatest impurities and has the most strenuous cleansing procedure. If you ate something impure it could only keep you from eating the Holy Temple sacrifices until that evening. This impurity means that a person cannot go into the Temple and eat from the sacrifices. It does not mean that a person is basically evil or dirty. If you ate pork or other impure foods you are automatically pure by evening time. (see Lev 11:40) Therefore, speaking evil is a much more serious impurity than eating unclean things as Mark 7:21 states. Yeshua is basing His teaching on this case and is making His bold statement that what a person takes out of his mouth does defile him. What comes out the mouth - criticism and evil talk - can be tantamount to leprosy which is the greatest impurity and for which one has to leave the camp. Even after a person thinks that he is healed it takes the priest some two weeks to declare him pure (Lev 14). All that the disciples did was not following the custom of a small Pharisaic group of extremists. But the Pharisees broke the teaching of the Law about vain condemnation of your fellow brothers which is a much more serious and direct commandment from the Law.

The Pharisees were offended when they heard this last statement - so the disciples of Yeshua told him. He answered: "Every plant which My heavenly Father did not plant shall be rooted up." This is a classic Pharisaic statement. In fact, we have one of the great teachers of the Pharisees, Gamaliel, making the same teaching in Act 5:34-40. Vs.38-39,

> *"And so in the present case, 1 say to you, stay away from these men and let them alone, for if this plan or action should be of men, it will be overthrown; but if it is of God, you will not be able to overthrow them; or else you may even be found fighting against God."*

Again on this point, we can see the close affinity of Yeshua and the Pharisees. The arguments which the Pharisees had with Yeshua were arguments of people who had common interests and goals. The spiritual diseases which Yeshua pointed out to the Pharisees of the first century have also found their way into the "Christian Churches" and have even nested there and bore offspring.

WHERE DO YOU COME FROM?

From Teaching from Zion, Vol. 1 No 16, July 1986

On the gate of the Athenian pavilion in Delphi, Greece the rock bears a Greek inscription which in English would be translated "know thy self". This statement later on became an important rabbinical teaching.

Rabbi Akiva Ben-Mahalal says:

> *"see three things and you will preserve*
> *yourself from sin. Know where you come*
> *from, where you are going and in front*
> *of whom you are going to be judged."*

It should be noted that although the rabbis used the Greek statement, they actually used it as a polemic against the Greek way of thinking. This is clear from the answer that the rabbis gave to this statement.

> *"Where do you come from? From a sordid*

*drop! Where are you going? To the place
of dust, worm, and rot! In front of whom
will you be judged? In front of the King
of Kings the Holy One blessed be He!"*

However, the reason that I wrote the above is because it is time for us to deal with these very questions in respect to our work in "Netivyah". Where are we coming from?

In 1972 seven people met in our home and talked about the situation of the "Christian" groups in Israel at the time. The situation in 1972 was sad and difficult. Many churches had missions and missionaries in Israel. Each one of these missionaries was peddling his particular brand of "church" and "creed". Not a single one of those missionaries in Jerusalem wanted to see the Man of Galilee in the light of the first century Jewish context. They all came to Israel from America, U.K., Canada, Germany, etc. with a well packaged and refurbished Jesus made in Rome, Canterbury, Cleveland, or Amsterdam.

The seven of us in 1972 made a decision to do everything possible in order to establish a local Israeli first century congregation of Jews who knew that Yeshua is the Messiah. Each of us had a different starting point. Three came from an Orthodox Jewish background, one was an American raised in the church of Christ, two of us were secular Israeli Jews, and one was a Finnish woman married to an Orthodox Jew. We knew where we came from.

Where we are going is more important. Two things were totally clear to us.

First, none of us wanted to go back to his "old ways" - to the time before we found the Messiah.

Second, none of the seven wanted us to become like the protestant evangelical churches in Jerusalem. Rather, we wanted to rediscover Jesus from the root upward.

When the State of Israel was about to be inaugurated, Berl Katzenelson said:

> *"A generation of renewal creates, it does not pitch into the rubbish the inheritance of past generations. He checks, tests, chooses, and rejects. There are times that he holds onto an old tradition and improves on it. At other times he goes down into the garbage cans of the past and salvages things long forgotten, cleans them up from their rusty past, raises from the dead the old ways and feeds the new generation with the strength of the old."*

This is where "Netivyah" is going to! We want to bring the crown of the King Messiah back to Israel and to the Jewish people. We are daily working toward the establishment of God's spiritual Kingdom here on earth - until He comes!

In front of whom are we going to be judged?

This question, of course, has a simple profound answer:

> *"Because He (God) has fixed a day in which He will judge the world in righteousness through a Man whom He (God) has appointed, having furnished proof to all men by raising Him from the dead". (Acts 17:31. See also Acts 10:42.)*

Yeshua the Messiah will judge the whole world. Knowing this, of course, is absolutely essential for our lives on earth. However, the more important aspect of this Biblical fact is its implications. God, through Yeshua, will be our judge and to him we ought to give account. We, therefore, should not fear the judgments of men.

"Netivyah" is thus an organization seeking to fear God and not men - be it Jewish Orthodox zealots or self- righteous Christians who think that God's world revolves around their particular doctrine and sectarian church. We truly want to be free from all bondages. Therefore, we truly want to know the truth. This is the essence of the Restoration Movement. The Lord has blessed us with the people and tools to be able to look for the

Biblical truth and find it in His Holy Bible. This is "Netivyah"!

This is our understanding of the questions "where do you come from, where are you going to, and in front of whom will you be judged?". It is not a pessimistic understanding. But it is the expectation and high hope for the future of the Jewish people and the body of Christ.

A short news report from "Netivyah": The Shulam family has finally been completed by the Lord. Our daughter, Danah, obeyed the Gospel and was immersed in a spring of water outside of Jerusalem in the Judaean desert on the last Wednesday of the month of May. Danah is fourteen years old and made her decision to obey the Gospel strictly on her own. We have never pressured our children into any kind of religious constraint but have given them the right and the tools to choose what they want to do with their lives. This, of course, makes it doubly more-gratifying to us. Danah after having studied the Bible extensively came to a decision that Yeshua truly is the Messiah, the Son of God and that she wanted to give her life to him. We have seen a marked change in Danah after her baptism - in little things that were difficult for her before. We hope that the Lord and His Holy Spirit will continue to guide her and the rest of us in the Shulam family to be obedient to Him and give in His Service.

On the sixth-of June we had another baptism, this time in the Jordan River, of a dear sweet lady who has been taking care of the children of one of our families here in "Netivyah ". She comes from a very long line of rabbinical Orthodox families and it was a very difficult decision for her, as it is for many Jewish people, to accept Yeshua as her Messiah. Finally, after she attended and saw the baptism of my daughter, she also made up her mind to obey the Gospel. Last Friday we took her to the River and there she was immersed in the Mashiach.

Project, Rabbi Teach Us, is now going full steam ahead. We have Hilary Le Cornu, a doctoral candidate at the Hebrew University in Comparative Religion and Baruch Berkovitz, a former rabbinical student, who are working on the project. They are both members of our congregation here in Jerusalem. Also working with us is Dr. Brad Young, who has just received his doctorate from Professor David Flusser in the area of New Testament and Judaic Studies in the intertestamental and first century period. This, including myself, is the crew who is working on the project.

The only weak point in this project is the financial side.' In spite of the fact that many of you people have contributed liberally and willingly to the project, we have not covered our expenses. Actually, the only expense that we have, at this point, is the salaries of the people who are working. Brad is getting a $1000 a month gross since he already has his doctorate. Hilary and Baruch are each getting about $400 a month gross. Even though Baruch and Hilary are working quite hard, they are willing to accept a lesser salary at this time since they have fewer needs. Even so, we have not been able to make the bills for these salaries every month. We are praying to God that either foundations, trusts, churches, or people who have funds and believe that such a commentary which has the Jewish background and first century Jewish correlation to the New Testament is important will somehow find a way to help if it is their desire.

This summer I will be traveling in the United States. At this point, I have 65 days of back-to-back 'lectures. This is a very heavy load. I will need your prayers. I will probably see many of you during my trip that will start in Nashville, Tennessee and end up in Washington, D.C. after Georgia, Oregon, Alaska, California, and Texas. So I really hope that you will pray for me.

ISRAEL IN MESSIANIC PERSPECTIVE

From Teaching from Zion Vol. 1 No 17 September 1986

Israel is a country accustomed to miracles. Every significant event in our 4000 years of history has been accompanied by signs and wonders. Even Moses, after the burning bush, asked for a sign to accompany his return to Egypt. Can you imagine a state like Israel surviving without some kind of unexplainable super-mundane events to accompany its existence? Personally, I cannot!

The government of Israel is made up of thirteen different parties - which include the left and right wings - and in between are the orthodox Jewish parties who bribe both sides to get what they want. In the last election, over thirty political parties ran for election. Now the surprise. Today, Mr. Shimon Peres, from the Israel Labor Party, is turning the Prime Minister's seat over to Isaac Shamir from the Likud party, which is and has been the opposition for over thirty years. This step down of Mr. Peres is not on the basis of election but on the basis of a previous agreement signed over two years ago. Both parties, who have opposed each other for over thirty years, made an agreement to share the running of the government during a four-year period half and half for the sake of the national good.

In other words, both parties were willing to put their private views and preferences aside for the wellbeing of the nation as a whole. Everyone in Israel has waited for one of the parties to renege on the agreement and not hand over the Prime Minister's seat to the opposition. Most would not have been surprised to see this happen. But, we are all surprised to see Mr. Peres step down to the Foreign Minister's office and give Mr. Shamir the Prime Minister's seat.

Following are things that we can learn from this unique political move:

First, putting the good of the nation as a whole over and above personal party good.

Second, keeping our word and agreements even when it hurts. Politicians in the whole world, and especially in Israel, have not been known to have the highest moral standards. However, this last example could serve, for all of us, as a "sign and wonder" to point to higher grounds.

MISSION WORK IN ISRAEL — A NEW DAWN

From Teaching from Zion Vol 1 No 18 April 1986

At the time of the great empires of the west, a great surge of missionary activity took wings in all western denominations. Most of the emphasis was on Africa. But, some missionaries also came to the Middle-East and tried their fortune in bringing the Gospel to both Muslims and Jews. The Jewish population was small and poor. It was mostly centered around the Jewish historical holy places. Jerusalem was one of those centers in which the Jewish population was dense and poor. The Jews of Jerusalem were largely Orthodox and lived from the different Jewish welfare agencies who were sent funds from abroad. There were a few small Jewish business ventures and artisans. But for the most part, the major financial oxygen came from people like Baron Rothschild, Baron Montefiore, and the like. The "Christian" missions moved into this situation in a big way. The English Church especially moved with a great zeal into the scene, building schools, hospitals, and sending in well trained men.

Some of the people that they sent were Jews who had converted to Christianity. One of the most prominent was Bishop Alexander who built "Christ's Church" at the Jaffa gate just inside the Old City. The first era of "Christian" missions in Israel was a period of acquisition of property and construction of buildings. Those churches that were here at that time really bought prime land in what is now the city center of Jerusalem. They bought this land for very little money because it was a ways from the Old City of Jerusalem and it was mostly unfit for farming. Today the same land is well worth millions of dollars. In fact, the English church in Jerusalem recently sold a small fraction of the land which they own in downtown Jerusalem for a sum of five million dollars to a wealthy Orthodox Jewish businessman.

No permanent work was left from any of the hundreds of missionaries who traversed this land at the turn of the century. But, beautiful buildings were left in Jerusalem by these missionaries.

The second period of missions in Israel began after the establishment of the State of Israel. The big missionary societies and formal churches received a certain air of respectability and had to depend on the Jewish State of Israel for their visa and entrance permits. They had official contact with the Ministry of Religious Affairs and could no longer openly evangelize. They had to disguise their missionary work with all kinds of services that would not be considered directly evangelistic. Some of the missions thus opened schools, kindergartens, book stores, art galleries, guest houses, etc...

Through these instruments some evangelism was going on with people who either worked for these institutions or received benevolent help from them. But, very little real ideological teaching took place in the land. Some Jewish people did assent to the Gospel. With the vast number of immigrants from Europe also came a rather sizable group of Jews who for one reason or another converted to Christianity through the Christian relief organizations who worked with Jews after the Holocaust. Most of these people were from eastern Europe and especially from Romania. They soon became connected with the missionaries from the particular denominations which they knew from abroad and formed little churches of the same nature and character that they had known in their respective countries.

This formed a kind of Christian ghetto. The people in that ghetto had a dual identity. Inside their church they were "Christian" and outside the church they were Jews. At home, many of them led a secular Jewish life. In the church they worshiped just like they did in Europe with the same songs and even in the same language. The Israeli Jewish community did not even get a whiff of real witness from most of these little communities that dotted the land of Israel. The Orthodox Jewish organizations, who set for themselves a goal to fight against Christians, gave trouble from time to time.

These little groups lived in great fear that some person might find out that they were "Christian" and cause trouble for them in their job or neighborhood. The work that the churches of Christ did in Israel in the early sixties was not much different from the situation described above. The churches of Christ had an additional disadvantage. They did not have a record of caring for Jewish people in the post-World War II period, nor did they have any experience prior to the early sixties of working with Jews. This caused a great problem and attracted even less desirable characters than those who hung around the denominations which had buildings, property, and some history in this place.

Israeli and Jewish evangelism in the world is now beginning to undergo a thorough reformation. Jewish believers are no longer ashamed of their Jewishness. I remember in a seminar that was held in the Manhattan church of Christ some years ago a dear brother, who is very well known in the church, revealed that he comes from a Jewish background, but had not mentioned this for twenty years. This brother thought that he gained some favor with Yeshua for not mentioning that he came from a Jewish family. I personally have strong doubts that Yeshua is pleased that Jews convert to Christianity and lose their identity. This, of course, is in direct opposition to I Cor.7:17-21, which states that,

> *"if you were called from the circumcision do not seek to become uncircumcised..."*

The reader might ask why this point is important. Well, it is important because the new Jewish believer in Christ does not have to live a double life. He can hold onto his Jewish background as something to be proud of and not ashamed of. Only when a person has some positive pride in who he is ethnically and nationally can he also have pride in who he is spiritually. The new Jewish believers in Israel have more boldness and courage to stand up for Yeshua Ha- Messiah.

There is a correlation between a personal security in one's own identity and the Gospel. The new spirit of evangelism in Israel is not being led by foreign missionaries. These missionaries are still, with a few exceptions, unable to relate to the Jewish population in Hebrew. And, they are still fearful for the legal status that their churches have in Israel. Although, it must be mentioned, many of the expatriate missionaries in Israel have accepted the role of supporters and facilitators for the Israeli brothers. The missionaries who have accepted this role have been most welcome and helpful in their work.

"Netivyah" has been fortunate to be among one of the first groups in Israel who has seen that Israeli evangelism will be most effective when it is done by Jews in the Jewish context of the Good News. When we started to sing Hebrew songs from the Psalms and Scripture in 1972, one of the leaders of the Jewish Hebrew Christians in Israel stated that these were not "Christian" songs. Today every congregation in Israel sings at least some of these same songs and many have written original new Jewish Christian songs. "Netivyah" has insisted for years that Jews ought to follow Paul's teaching and example of living as a Jew in Messiah yet at the same time giving our brothers the freedom of conscience to live as the Lord guides them in all matters of culture and ethnic practices which do not contradict the Word. This freedom in the Messiah includes things such as celebrating the national feasts, choices of food, and manner of dress. The claims that we had both then and now are that living within the people and with the people of Israel will give a great surge to local evangelism and indigenous congregations. We praise the Lord, Yeshua Ha-Messiah, that a decade later we see the fruit of our labor throughout the Land.

May the Lord God of Israel bless all of those who

support the teaching of the Word to the Jewish people. And, we especially bless all of you who pray for Israel's salvation. With much love to you in Yeshua.

Memo

A note of explanation might be in order for the readers who are not yet versed in the Jewish literature of the time of Yeshua. In the following article you will find references to a number of Jewish Rabbinic sources which are important for the understanding of the term "Power of God" in the context of First Century Judaism. These works, such as Midrash, which means a commentary in Rabbinic style dated between 200 BCE and 500 CE, or Qumran (Q), which is the place where the Dead Sea Scrolls were found. Do not let these terms intimidate you. You can still understand and appreciate the article and get a good idea of the inside workings of the First Century understanding of religious issues in the deep-rooted meaning of God's Word.

THE COMMENTARY PROJECT

From Teaching from Zion, Vol 1 no 19 December 1987

"Netivyah" has had a hard year in many respects. However, when I say hard it does not mean a "bad" year it means that things did not really turn out as well, healthy, or as quickly as I would have wished for them to turn out or happen. But, if I look back, when have we had an "easy" year in Israel? Let me share with you the status of some of our main projects.

THE CONTRIBUTIONS OF THE HEBREW COMMENTARY ON THE NEW TESTAMENT:

The commentary project was started in May of 1985 with Rabbi Menachem Rubin working on the Gospel of Matthew. After a few months of working with Rabbi Rubin it became evident that we would have a hard time working together. The main reason why we terminated the working relationship with Rabbi Rubin was that his production was slow. Less than one chapter a month was being produced. In the contract we had spoken of more than two chapters per month. After Rabbi Rubin stopped working for us we hired Dr. Brad Young, who has his PhD from the Hebrew University.

Dr. Young did not want to continue working on Matthew - although we already had four chapters of Matthew finished. Dr. Young felt that Rabbi Rubin's style was so different from his that it would be inadvisable to continue. Dr. Young thus started to work on Luke. He worked for a course of four months eight hours a day. We soon learned that Rabbi Rubin did work hard and did produce good material but that we were too ambitious and demanding of him and that it was really impossible to do a good job in primary research any faster.

Now, we have Dr. Young working for us and being paid only for what he produces. Doctoral candidate, Hilary Le Cornu, joined our team working full time in the office and on the commentary. We have all worked exceedingly hard on this commentary but the rate of progress is much slower than we anticipated. This has frustrated me greatly and at times has even discouraged me from continuation - especially during the times when we did not know how we would pay the salary of those who labor with us. (We must be thankful that in the last few months we had no immediate financial problems with this project. The Osaka Christian Assembly - provided a generous gift earmarked for the commentary project.) But, now as I make my accounting before God and man, as a steward of the Kingdom, it is clear to me that the contributions that the commentary research have already made are of significance - even when the number of chapters that have been finished arc few.

All this I said as a way of introduction for a short list of contributions made by the scholars at work on this commentary project. The form of this list will be in the "Did you Know" style.

1. **DID YOU KNOW** that in 1984 a stone Ossuary (a box made from stone or pottery for secondary burial during the second temple period) from the first century was purchased by the Israel Antiquities department? The ossuary had this inscription on it: "Yohana the daughter of Yohanan ("John" in Anglo-Saxon languages) the son of Theophilos the High Priest." We say this in regard to "Theophilos" to whom the Gospel of Luke and the Book of Acts are dedicated.

2. **DID YOU KNOW** that Jewish people do not give a name to their sons until the eighth day at the time of circumcision? The oldest record of this custom is in the New Testament - Luke 1:59-63. Zechariah gave his son a name during the circumcision ceremony just like Jews

do in our own days.

3.   **DID YOU KNOW** that the words "consolation of Israel " in the prayer of Simon the Just (Luke 2:25) are based on Isaiah 40:Iff, "Comfort Ye, Comfort Ye my People Said the Lord "? The word "Consolation" in Luke is a Greek translation of the Hebrew word "Nachamu" which means to "comfort", "console", "repent"... In the New Testament "The consolation of Israel" is the coming of Yeshua the Messiah.

4.   **DID YOU KNOW** that God did not reject Israel when He gave his only begotten Son to die for our sins? "I say then, Hath God cast away (reject) his people? God forbid. For I also am an Israelite, of the seed of Abraham, of the tribe of Benjamin." "As concerning the gospel, they are enemies for your sakes: but as touching the election, they are beloved for the father's sake. For the gifts and calling of God are without repentance." (Romans 11:1, 28-29.)

5.   **DID YOU KNOW** that in Qumran the "Essenes" in their commentary on the book of Habakkuk which they called "pesher", interpret the verse speak of "The righteous shall live by Faith" (Hab. 2:4)in a very close way to the Pauline writings? Here, too, it is through faith in a person, the Teacher of Righteousness, that the community expected redemption. In the pesher on Habakkuk, the author interprets

2.4 thus: "The explanation of this concerns all those who observe the Law in the house of Judah. God will deliver them from the house of judgment because of their affliction and their faith in the Teacher of Righteousness." (IQS 3.2, 7-8. Of., too, 1 Tim.4.8.) Paul was not alone in his interpretation of Hab. 2: 4, the Qumran community over 100 years before Paul interpreted this verse in the same way.

These are just some very small things which come from the commentary. They are not major findings but they do give insight into the Jewishness of the New Testament text. And, this is what our work with the commentary is supposed to do - is going to be, Lord willing, the only New Testament commentary in Hebrew and it should revive the Hebrew background of the teachings of the Apostles.

The above example gives you a cursive glimpse into our work. From time to time we will publish small portions of our work in English especially for those who support this project so that you will be able to share in our joy. We do need your support - this year most of the support for this work came from Japan (Osaka Christian Assembly), a group of people who are very serious about learning the Word of God. We want other brothers and sisters to share in this great blessing.

WHY DID THE JEWISH LEADERS NOT ACCEPT YESHUA AS THE MESSIAH?

From Teaching from Zion, Vol 1 no 19 December 1987

Introduction:

The question that this lecture deals with is one which has occupied the relationship of Jews and Yeshua for two thousand years. If Yeshua is the Messiah for whom Israel waits and yearns, the acceptance of Him will be a source of the greatest joy to God. It is clear to all people with a thinking mind, that Yeshua is not a subject which can be ignored. In the West, at least, Yeshua confronts the Jewish community with both great amazement and solicitude. On the one hand Yeshua is thought of as the cause of all the troubles that Jews have had all the years of the diaspora. On the other hand, Yeshua has been the prime mover in western civilization toward a domestication of the wiles of paganism. The great cultural achievements of the west are all empowered by the character and genius of this lone Galilean.

Body:

I. The Messiah in Jewish expectations.

A. The two-fold expectations of the Messiah in Old Testament Judaism.

1.) The National political expectations, which embodied themselves in the liberation of Israel from oppressing enemies. And, dominion over the nations around - even the whole world.

2) The Spiritual - Redemptive - atoning for the sin aspect of the Messiah. It is obvious that both aspects are interwoven as one fabric in Jewish thought, but none the less they are two separate and distinct ideas. In some chapters of Jewish History one or the other of these two distinct ideas received prominence. Most of the time, especially in times of oppression the National political aspects were much more conspicuous than the spiritual. The Jewish Rabbis actually were willing to ignore every precaution, and disregard every requirement for the sake of any political lallygag. This is why the great and esteemed Rabbi Akiva, could make Bar Kochba a messiah, even though he was not from the House of David, and did not excel in keeping the law, and did not fulfill

any of the expected messianic prophecy. What Bar-Kocheba did have, however, was the political and military zeal that gave the impression to the Jewish Rabbis that deliverance from the Roman oppressor is coming from Bar-Kochba.

B. The Spiritual aspects of the Jewish messianic vision was not totally ignored most of the time. However, they received greater prominence only after the destruction of the Temple and the quenching of the second revolt. In other words, only when hope for a political national messianic intervention failed, did the Rabbis give much attention to the spiritual promises of God connected to the Messiah. This would be clear to see in the Midrashic telling of Messianic stories. The above reason is one of the main reasons why Jewish people have been so relatively easy to accept false messiahs like Sabbetai Zvi and Shelomo Molcho...etc.

II.   The Biblical definition of our messianic expectations.

A. From the House of David. Isaiah 11:1,10

B. Will forgive sin. Isaiah 53:5

C. Will make the nations come to Jerusalem. Isaiah 60:5f

1.The nations will come of their own will to worship in Jerusalem.

2. Those who do not will have problems

with supernatural character. Zech. 14

3. There will be a Victory in the end, but it will not be affected by the strength and expertise of the Jewish people. Ezk.39 (We see the fulfillment of this passage in the Revelation of John, the end of the kingdom of evil.)

4. Justice and Mercy will be the general itinerary for all mankind. This of course does not mean that a powerful administration of these values will be the motivating factor in this general good behavior of all people. If this was so, any powerful dictator could produce such values for a period of time.

5. The Messiah was to bring the knowledge of God to all mankind, and abolish idolatry. This spiritual aspect did not get a sufficient place in the repertoire of Jewish messianic expectations.

III.   How did Yeshua the Messiah fit in this picture of Messianic Jewish Expectations.

A. John 18:36 "My Kingdom is not of this world".

1. The point that Yeshua makes with Pontius Pilatus is very obvious: If my kingdom was of this world I would have to use means of this world to accomplish the purposes of this worldly kingdom.

IT IS NOT POSSIBLE TO MAKE THINGS

OF THE HEAVENS WITH MEANS OF THIS EARTH.

2. The Earth is doomed for destruction. The world has no hope for eternity. The messianic kingdom cannot be built on the means of this world and what it offers. I believe that if our people would somehow understand this point and stop relying and trusting ourselves, relying instead upon God, we would recognize the importance of Yeshua. (see John 6:15, and Matt.26:53)

3. Luke 17:20-21:

"The Kingdom of God is not coming with
signs to be observed; nor will they say,
'Look here it is!' or, 'There it is!'. For behold,
the kingdom of God is in your midst."

The Torah gives a clear indication that God's kingship over his people is not a question of Land, although Land is important; it is not a question of political system, although God has given us a political system by our request so that we can be like everyone else. (see I Sam.9) We sing the song from Deut.30:14 as an indication of the great spiritual kingdom over which God is King, and people are his subjects.

B. John 17:3 The messianic Kingdom cannot be some military global war which will superimpose peace in the world with the force of generals and captains, and a superior race which will dictate to the billions of white, yellow, and red, and black servants the daily orders of work, food, and activity. This picture sounds too much like *"Animal Farm"* by George Orwell, and not like the picture of Isaiah the prophet.

Conclusion:

We as Jews and as "Netivyah" need to understand the spiritual aspect of the Messianic Kingdom. The kingdom of the Messiah is something which is here with us now!!! In Mark 9:1 Yeshua promised that the Kingdom would come in The lifetime of the apostles, and we know that it did come. The lives of the Apostles themselves changed, and people's lives are changing now.

Would you not give up the hopeless search for a worldly kingdom, which blinds the eyes of our Rabbis and politicians, and make the real kingdom of God a reality in your own life? Come and die to this world and live forever with God, Yeshua and the saints.

WHAT'S HAPPENING
IN ISRAEL

From Teaching from Zion, Vol 1 no 21 November 1988

The Jewish Holy Days are a real special season in Jerusalem. A person can feel them coming on from the middle of August. Jerusalem becomes quiet and the streets are empty early in the evening. The people of Jerusalem start to prepare for the Holidays even a week before. The markets are full of goods, and the people are rushing about with baskets full of food and kitchen ware to decorate the festive tables. Although there are these expectations for the feasts, everyone is happy to see them behind them. Now the Holidays are finished, and we can get back to a long stretch of work, and a more or less regular schedule of activities.

In this "Teaching from Zion", I will share with you all some of the latest events and concerns that have come our way in the last few months. The order will be from the most recent past to the summer events.

When great things happen to the church, Satan cannot stand it. We learn this from John 16:20,

> *"Verily, verily, I say unto you, That ye shall weep and lament, but the world shall rejoice: and ye shall be sorrowful, but your sorrow shall be turned into joy."*

When the Body of the Messiah weeps and laments the world rejoices. And, when the church rejoices the world cannot stand it. This last month has been a great mixture of heavenly joy and great sorrow for Satan. But Satan has not been sitting idle. We have some casualties. In this newsletter I will share with you some of the great things that have happened this month, and also some of the arrows of evil that have struck us. If we could only understand this principle, our lives for God would be much more dedicated, and we would be much more careful to walk in God's ways.

In 1970, I wanted to publish a small article and ad in the Israeli Hebrew newspapers. Everyone said that it would be impossible. But I went full of confidence from God to the editor of Israel's largest newspaper, and submitted my article. The editor looked at me and said: "Are you a Jew?" I answered, "Yes!" "Do you believe in Jesus?" he asked. "I do," was my answer. "I will publish your ad just one time, one time only," the editor said. From this five-inch square ad in 1970 we published our correspondence courses that gave us the first contacts. Since that ad in 1970 we have had nothing published in the Israeli press. In fact, none of the Christians have had access to the Israeli Hebrew newspapers.

In the first week of September, we organized a five-day seminar on Evangelism. I headed the Lausanne committee team that did the seminar. We did not have as many people participate because the time was just a few days after the school year started. But, in spite of the small number, the seminar was a success. Evangelism was the only subject, and the practical issues were the main emphasis. One of the things that happened in this seminar was cooperation in writing a major article that would be attempted to be published in the largest Hebrew paper. We did not know if it would be possible to publish this article, but we prayed about it, and by faith Jacob Damkani, who took a major part in writing and financing the first article, went to the publisher of **Yediot Acharonot** the largest Hebrew paper that has over 450,000 copies printed every day, and on Friday over half a million.

The article was published. A full page. The title was **"Who is the Sacrifice?"** The whole Gospel of Yeshua our Messiah was written in the second publication of this article. The second publication was more sophisticated, and it had the story of salvation written in a sort of indirect way. In all three newspapers, a line-drawing of a lamb on the altar, made by Elhanan from our congregation, graced the center of the article. You should all understand that this is the first major media evangelism in Israel. The article outlined the great need for salvation and atonement of sin. This was done in a very Israeli way. The article then gave the answer for our sins, Yeshua the Messiah. Practical instruction of how to get saved was offered at the end of the article.

The amazing thing was that after **_Yediot Acharonot_** published the article, two other newspapers called Jacob, and asked him if he would like to publish the same article in their papers. They gave such a good price that it was possible to publish the articles. In ten days over 250 positive calls and letters were received. Every request is answered immediately with a letter and some basic literature about New Testament faith. Then, after a few days a phone call follows. We in Jerusalem get to follow up the Jerusalem area calls and contacts. These are great times. It seems that God has opened a way to use the Israeli media for the Kingdom's sake. Such opportunities have not been available to us until now. We must take advantage of them. Israel, in this present time, needs as much of the teaching of Yeshua the Messiah as possible. The Messiah is the only hope of breaking the cycle of violence. When God gives us opportunities we must take advantage of them.

Right now, I have these teachings going:

Sunday
   A Bible study from 4:30-6:30 pm.

Tuesday
   A study with some new contacts between 3:30-5:00 pm.

Thursday
   a) A study of First Century Biblical Exegesis for leaders of the Beit- Immanuel Messianic congregation in Tel-Aviv from 5:00-7:00 pm.
   b) A study with some Israeli unbelievers who have been involved in some strange cult, and are now interested in the Biblical New Testament faith.

Saturday
   The main worship service and teaching in our congregation in Jerusalem. In addition to these there are a number of private Bible studies with individuals going on each week.

The second great thing that has happened this month is the Jerusalem march. Last year 73 Jews wearing T-Shirts with the inscription, "Yeshua is the Messiah" marched. This year during the Feast of Booths Jerusalem march 210 people came to wear these T-Shirts and march.

The Orthodox organized a demonstration against

us. About 50 of the Orthodox came with posters and banners written with slogans against us, and even with quotations from the New Testament. The police asked them to leave, but they would not. Finally the police arrested, with violence, 20 of them, and broke their posters. This is the first time in public that the police has given a real fair protection to us, as Jewish believers in Yeshua.

The Israeli police, in public, in front of newspaper reporters and cameraman, came to the help of Jewish believers. Some people whom I knew, came up to me during the march and said: "Now you have come out of the closet." It was a great witness of the courage and new boldness of the Body of Christ in Israel. With God's help we are breaking the psychological barrier of fear. The brothers living in Israel have been afraid to come out in front of a hostile public and proclaim Yeshua as the Messiah. The fear was well founded. Now, however, this fear is being overcome. I wish that all of you could overcome the same fear.

Now some of the bad things that have happened in this month.

Because of our new found boldness the Orthodox have re-opened their court case against "Netivyah". They have pushed the city to make things quick, and the date for the court has been set for probably sometime in November or December, 1988. We will need your prayer and support for this case. We cannot continue the momentum and the fight without your help. This help has been coming with God's grace, and we have been waiting for such a time as this.

The future holds a lot of difficult times for us from an emotional, spiritual, and persecution standpoint. Please, help us see the Seed of the Kingdom give fruit in the land of Israel. Please continue to help us financially. There is just no way right now for us to continue these efforts of preaching the Good News to this war-torn part of the world without YOUR help. Envy is a sin, and we do not want to sin. But, when we see the dedication and support that denominational "missions' ' receive in Israel, and the relative amount of service that they render, we are almost driven to envy, but we hardly succumb to it.

In the beginning of the summer we started plans for a team of Israeli Jewish brothers who either live in Israel now, or can come back to Israel and live here without a visa problem. We wanted this team to be made up of people who are between twenty-five and thirty years old, married, and who have worked successfully in the world. These young people will not have any problems with language, or their ability to stay in Israel. They need no training in understanding the culture, and they do not need to live on American salaries. We have raised 500 dollars for Rami, who is one of these young men. A doctor in Nashville is providing this support for one year. But, we still need the support of others. With God's help we will soon have a team of young Israeli families who will witness the Good News to Israel. We need your help.

The "Rabbi Teach us Commentary" project is doing well. PhD candidate Ms. Hilary Le Cornu has been working eight to ten hours per day on this project, Lord Willing, in the next report I will share with you some more of the commentary work.

For most of the summer I was in the U.S.A, visiting congregations, doing some teaching and wishfully hoping to raise some much-needed funds for "Netivyah". The teaching that I did in places like Nashville, Abilene and California, was well accepted. For most people in the church many of the things about the Jewish background of the New Testament are new, and therefore they were not easy for them to accept, or evaluate. But in spite of these difficulties it seems that many did open their hearts, and minds to hear from the Word of the Lord. However, financially the summer trip was less successful.

There were some brothers who understood what it costs to travel across the Atlantic Ocean, and inside the U.S. We thank God for all the people whom we visited, and had a chance to break the bread of life with, and we hope that next time we come the Lord will bless us even more spiritually, and also materially. This I say not for my own sake, but for the sake of the important, and unique work that is being done in the land of Israel.

P.S. Barry is doing well at A.C.U. He is lonely and has not made many friends yet, but he is keeping up with his school work. He has a job for about two months, but the Boss required him to work too many hours. Barry chose to leave this too demanding job so that he could keep up with the school work and grades.

WHOM GOD HAS FOREKNOWN HE ALSO PREDESTINED... ROMANS 8:29-33

From Teaching from Zion, Vol 1 No 22 May 1989

Introduction:

Chapter 8 of the Letter to the Romans has supplied strength and spiritual guidance to many generations written and expounded from this chapter about the Holy Spirit and about the victorious life of the Christian for whom "all things work together for the good". In this lesson we want to examine two things that have received little attention within this standard exegesis: the relationship of chapter 8 to the following section (Romans 9-11) which deals with the relationship of Israel to the body of Messiah; b) the historical context of Rom.8.29- 3 and within the Pauline corpus as a whole.

The general context of this passage in Romans:

I. In Romans 7, Paul gives a very personal expression of the need for Yeshua's intervention in human nature. Only in Yeshua does there exist the possibility of conquering sin's mortal grip on the human being so that the believer can dedicate himself to the life of the spirit of God. In chapter 8, he explicates the role of the Holy Spirit in this process of victory that is in the Messiah. It is clear from the letter as a whole, but especially from this chapter, that the Body of the Messiah is under persecution: vs.18, "For I consider that the sufferings of this present time are not worthy to be compared with the glory that is to be revealed to us..." Vss. 24-24, which speaks of hope for salvation, seem to have an underlying tone of the need for perseverance. The end of the chapter also makes clear that these people were going through some hard times, even under the threat of death (Rom.8:36 is a quotation from Psalm 44:22

II. The historical background of Rom.8 is therefore a very specific one of persecution of the believers in the mainstream Jewish community. The framework is thus established within the historical circumstances of Israel as the people of God. It would seem, therefore, that Paul is introducing in this passage of 8.29-33 a major thesis concerning Israel, an introduction to the famous chapters of 9-11 which is unanimously interpreted as Paul's thesis on

Israel's election and her relationship to the Gospel and the church.

III. A proposed exegesis for Romans 8:29-33: .1 The terminology used in Romans 8:29-33 is standard terminology used in the context of God's relationship with Israel.

(a) **"Called"** - (See Rom. 9:241, , 1Cor.1:24, Jude 1) This term is used in Paul's writing to signify the choice of God for the Jews and those from the Gentiles who have believed in the Messiah. In I Corinthians and Romans it is originally related to the Jewish people.

(b) **"Foreknow"** - (Se Eph. 1:5, 1 Pet. 1:22) The most convincing passage is ni Romans 11:2, which comes to affirm that God has not rejected Israel, and the argument is ni Verse 2, "God hasn't rejected His people whom He foreknew... "3

(c) **" Predestined "** - (Eph . 1:11", 3 : 1 1)

(d) **"Elect"** - (Luke 18:7, Romans 11:7,28) We see in chapter 11:7 that the "elect" are those Jews who have not been hardened from obtaining the Messiah.

The terms used here in this constellation correspond very closely in general context to Ephesians This would appear to indicate that Paul's subject here is not merely the personal walk of the individual in the Spirit, but has a special place as an introduction to the section of Romans

9-11.

The context is again Israel's relationship to God and their redemption from God. This is corroborated by the pronounal usage that Paul uses in consistent fashion throughout his letters. I believe that when Paul uses the first-person pronoun in plural he is referring to the Jewish believers. When Paul uses the second or third plural pronouns he is referring to the non-Jewish element in the church. This principle is very clear in Ephesians 1, but it is all through the Pauline epistles: vss. 12-18:

> "We (the Jewish believers) are under obligation,
> not to the flesh. For if you (the Gentiles) are
> living according to the flesh, you must die;
> but if by the Spirit you are putting to death
> the deeds of the body, you will live. For all
> (both Jew and Gentile) who are being led by
> the Spirit of God, these are sons of God."5

IV. The significance of this passage word for introduction to the famous chapters of 9-11

1. From vs. 12 onwards, Paul develops the theme of "sonship": the ability of calling God "Abba", and the personal obligation that comes from this relationship both to the sons and to the Father. The people are going through persecution. A challenge is laid before them to live according to the Spirit as

sons of God, because that is what they are. The way to do it is to suffer with the Messiah in order to the might also be glorified with Him. Paul is speaking to those who know the Torah..."), attempting to encourage them to hold on to their faith. In Vs. 25, we hear Paul's encouragement to keep up hope, although, at present they see no rational reason to do so. Now come the reasons why their hope ought to be strong and real:

2. Vs. 26, the Spirit of God helps our weakness.

(a) We do not even know how to pray, but the Spirit Himself intercedes for us.

(b) Vs. 28, we know that God is the primary cause of all things.' And, with God all things work for the good of His children who love Him and "who are called according to His purpose".

(c) Vs. 29, those whom God has foreknown, i.e. Israel, He also predestined to become the image of His Son. Why was it important to God, if He is the creator, t h a t people so bound by weakness be conformed to the glorious image of His Son? The reason is given in the second half of the verse: "that He might be the first born among many brethren." To understand this argument one has to put himself into the world Yeshua.

The first born is the one who inherits the father? There is no honor and glory in being the first born if you have no other brothers. God could not send the Messiah into a vacuum. He had to have a family, and a nation, and brothers.

(d) Vs. 30, if God predestined these brethren of His Son to conform to His image, it follows that He also called them. In Jewish thinking there is no Calvinistic "predestination". Predestination in Judaism does not forego the right of choice, and faithfulness. What it means is that God had prior knowledge that these people would live up to His expectations of them. In order for this predestination to work, a "call" still has to be given, which Israel can choose to hear or harden their hearts. Even if they harden their hearts, however, it does not mean that God has made a wrong judgment. It means that God has some plan to educate them, usually with punishment so that eventually they will come around and live up to His image in the Messiah. So if God "predestined" them, He also must have called them. And, whom God calls he also justifies, and if they obey He also glorified.

V. Paul from verse 31 on is confronting his opposition with rhetorical questions.

1. "If God is for us, who is against us?" -

What can a person say to God's "election", "foreknowledge" and "predestination"? God is for us, and all the persecution that we might experience means nothing because (vss. 35-39) we have the love of God, which at the end is for our Good.

2. God gave His own Son for us, why should we have any doubt that He will also give us all the things which He promised?

3. No one can bring a charge against God's elect because God is the one who justifies, He is the Judge. No one can condemn us, because the Messiah Yeshua died for us and raised from the dead sitting at the right hand of God, He also intercedes for us.

4. Can anything or person separate us from the Love of God which is in the Messiah Yeshua our Lord?

Conclusion:

It seems that this passage is used by Paul to introduce a major thesis about Israel's status in the eyes of God following His sending of the Messiah. The problem was that Israel in its majority did not accept the Messiah, and the Gentiles were also questioning the validity of Israel as a whole. The Jewish believers were somewhat discouraged by this situation because they were being persecuted both by the synagogue and the Gentiles. The ame promises that were made to those discouraged

Christians in the first century still stand good for us. We are still God's elect. We still face difficulty with discouragement. We are still being called by God to obedience in Yeshua His Son. But it is also still true that if God is for us, who can be against us. It is still true that no one can bring charges against God's elect.

It is still true that nothing can separate us from the Lord's love which is sufficient for us. We can take encouragement from Paul's encouragement of the early church and know that He has not rejected His people.

BOOKS IN THIS SERIES

Teaching from Zion - A Retrospective

The collection of Articles from Teaching from Zion Magazine.

Collection 1 - 1980S

Collection 2 - 1990S

Collection 3 - 2000S

Collection 4 - 2010S

Collection 5 - 2020S

Travel Edition - Collection 1 - 1980S

Travel Edition - Collection 2 - 1990S

Travel Edition - Collection 3 - 2000S

Travel Edition - Collection 4 - 2010S

Travel Edition - Collection 5 - 2020S

ABOUT THE AUTHOR

Joseph Shulam

Joseph Shulam is Director Emeritus of Netivyah Bible Instruction Ministry in Jerusalem Israel and President of Netivyah International. His unique persepctive as an Israeli Jewish Believer in the Messiah Yeshua has given him opportunity to lecture and teach the Good News worldwide. He has established messianic congregations in Israel, Brazil, Finland, Bulgaria, and the Far East. He holds degrees from the Hebrew University in Jerusalem and Lipscomb University in Nashville TN.

BOOKS BY THIS AUTHOR

Planted In The House Of The Lord

Hidden Treasures

From Jerusalem To Jerusalem

The Jewish Roots Of The Book Of Acts

The Jewish Roots Of The Book Of Romans

The Jewish Roots Of Galatians

Made in the USA
Columbia, SC
28 September 2024

42505642R00120